Contents

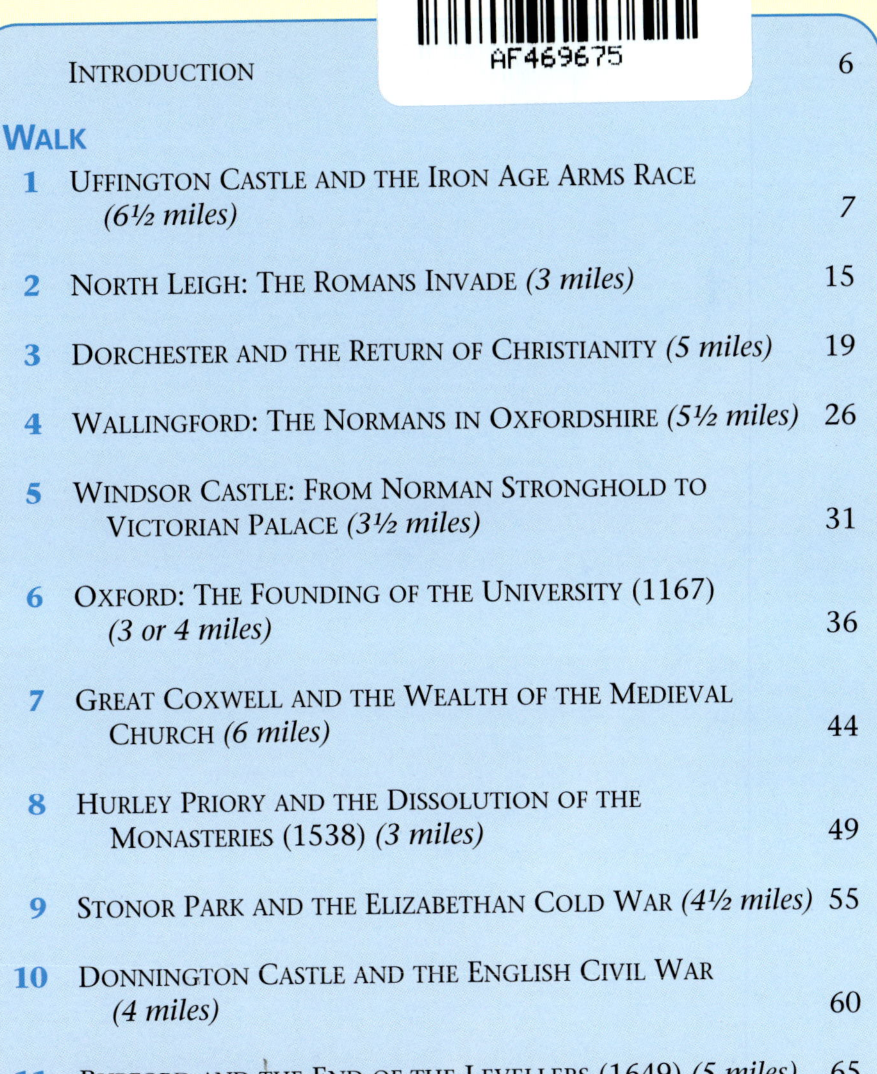

Introduction   6

WALK

1   Uffington Castle and the Iron Age Arms Race *(6½ miles)*   7

2   North Leigh: The Romans Invade *(3 miles)*   15

3   Dorchester and the Return of Christianity *(5 miles)*   19

4   Wallingford: The Normans in Oxfordshire *(5½ miles)*   26

5   Windsor Castle: From Norman Stronghold to Victorian Palace *(3½ miles)*   31

6   Oxford: The Founding of the University (1167) *(3 or 4 miles)*   36

7   Great Coxwell and the Wealth of the Medieval Church *(6 miles)*   44

8   Hurley Priory and the Dissolution of the Monasteries (1538) *(3 miles)*   49

9   Stonor Park and the Elizabethan Cold War *(4½ miles)*   55

10   Donnington Castle and the English Civil War *(4 miles)*   60

11   Burford and the End of the Levellers (1649) *(5 miles)*   65

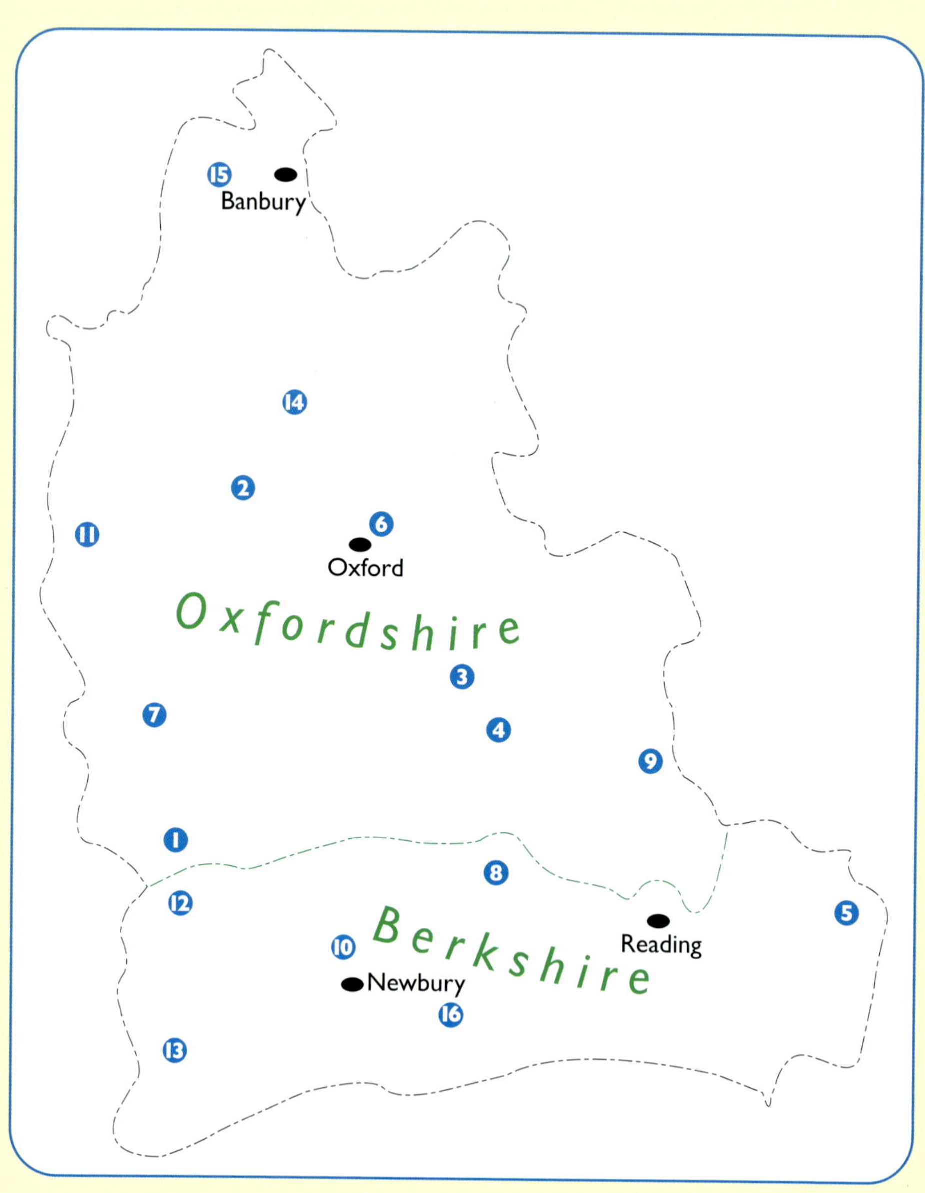

AREA MAP SHOWING LOCATION OF THE WALKS

WALKS INTO HISTORY

BERKSHIRE & OXFORDSHIRE

John Wilks

COUNTRYSIDE BOOKS
NEWBURY BERKSHIRE

First published 2008
© John Wilks, 2008

COUNTRYSIDE BOOKS
3 Catherine Road
Newbury, Berkshire

To view our complete range of books,
please visit us at
www.countrysidebooks.co.uk

ISBN 978 1 84674 069 5

Designed by Peter Davies, Nautilus Design

Produced through MRM Associates Ltd., Reading
Typeset by CJWT Solutions, St Helens
Printed in Thailand

WALK

12 ASHDOWN HOUSE AND THE WINTER QUEEN *(5½ miles)*   70

13 HUNGERFORD AND THE GLORIOUS REVOLUTION (1688)
     (5 miles)   75

14 BLENHEIM PALACE: HEYDAY OF THE FIRST CHURCHILLS
     (1704–1710) *(5 miles)*   81

15 WROXTON ABBEY AND THE AMERICAN WAR OF
     INDEPENDENCE (1756) *(4 miles)*   87

16 WOOLHAMPTON AND THE TRANSPORT REVOLUTION
     (5 miles)   92

PUBLISHER'S NOTE

We hope that you obtain considerable enjoyment from this book; great care has been taken in its preparation. Although at the time of publication all routes followed public rights of way or permitted paths, diversion orders can be made and permissions withdrawn.

We cannot, of course, be held responsible for such diversion orders and any inaccuracies in the text which result from these or any other changes to the routes nor any damage which might result from walkers trespassing on private property. We are anxious though that all details covering the walks are kept up to date and would therefore welcome information from readers which would be relevant to future editions.

The simple sketch maps that accompany the walks in this book are based on notes made by the author whilst checking out the routes on the ground. They are designed to show you how to reach the start, to point out the main features of the overall circuit and they contain a progression of numbers that relate to the paragraphs of the text.

However, for the benefit of a proper map, we do recommend that you purchase the relevant Ordnance Survey sheet covering your walk. The Ordnance Survey maps are widely available, especially through booksellers and local newsagents.

INTRODUCTION

Walking in Berkshire and Oxfordshire is a pleasure in all seasons. There is such a variety of landscape to discover, from the rolling downs on which Bronze Age man carved out a White Horse, to the water meadows of the river Thames. Quiet footpaths and country lanes through fields and woods, ancient trackways, canal towpaths and riverside walks take you for a while away from the cares and hurry of the modern world.

My twin passions are walking and history, and there can be few areas where such a rich heritage can be found and enjoyed on routes accessible to most walkers. The 16 walks in this book take you from the Iron Age to the Transport Revolution of the 18th and 19th centuries, with contrasts such as the hillfort at Uffington and our greatest royal residence, Windsor Castle; or Blenheim Palace, gift to a great general from a queen, and picturesque Burford, where ordinary soldiers dared to dream of a fairer world. There really is something here for everyone, including an exploration of the beautiful city of Oxford.

Each route has been chosen because it takes the walker past sites that reveal this rich and varied history. They vary in length between 3 and 6½ miles and all routes are circular, with grid references given for the starting point. Notes are provided on where refreshments can be obtained. Sketch maps are included, with numbered points corresponding to numbered paragraphs in the text, but it is recommended that you also carry the relevant Ordnance Survey map, details of which are given. There is also information on where to park but if you have to park on the road, please do so with consideration for other road users and take care not to block entrances or exits.

There is much to enjoy on these walks, so allow yourself plenty of time. Above all, I hope you enjoy these walks into history as much as I have done. Happy walking!

John Wilks

WALK 1
UFFINGTON CASTLE AND THE IRON AGE ARMS RACE

Length: 6½ miles

Wayland's Smithy

HOW TO GET THERE: The walk starts at the National Trust car park, approached up a minor road leading south off the B4507, 7 miles west of Wantage and 13 miles east of Swindon.

PARKING: The car park is clearly signposted for several miles along the B4507.

MAP: OS Landranger 174 (GR 294865).

INTRODUCTION

This is a very rewarding walk, although quite strenuous, and starts at atmospheric Uffington Castle hillfort before following the clear Ridgeway track along the downs past Wayland's Smithy, an ancient long barrow burial mound. It then descends to the plain beneath and goes through fields and along quiet lanes, past picturesque Compton Beauchamp country house and church, before climbing steeply back to the start past the White Horse and Dragon Hill.

HISTORICAL BACKGROUND

From 1000 BC onwards the climate across the British Isles deteriorated, becoming colder and wetter. The rising water-table made the soil of the downs too heavy and wet for growing crops and the inhabitants moved into the valleys of the Thames and Cherwell, just when the traditionally settled land in the river valleys was becoming exhausted after centuries of intensive farming. At the same time the population had increased dramatically, and there was growing competition for the available arable land.

   This movement and rising population coincided with the increased use of iron for tools and for weapons. Iron was easier to work than bronze, and iron ore was much more readily available. Consequently, iron weapons were used to settle the ever more frequent conflicts over land. For protection, families and tribes

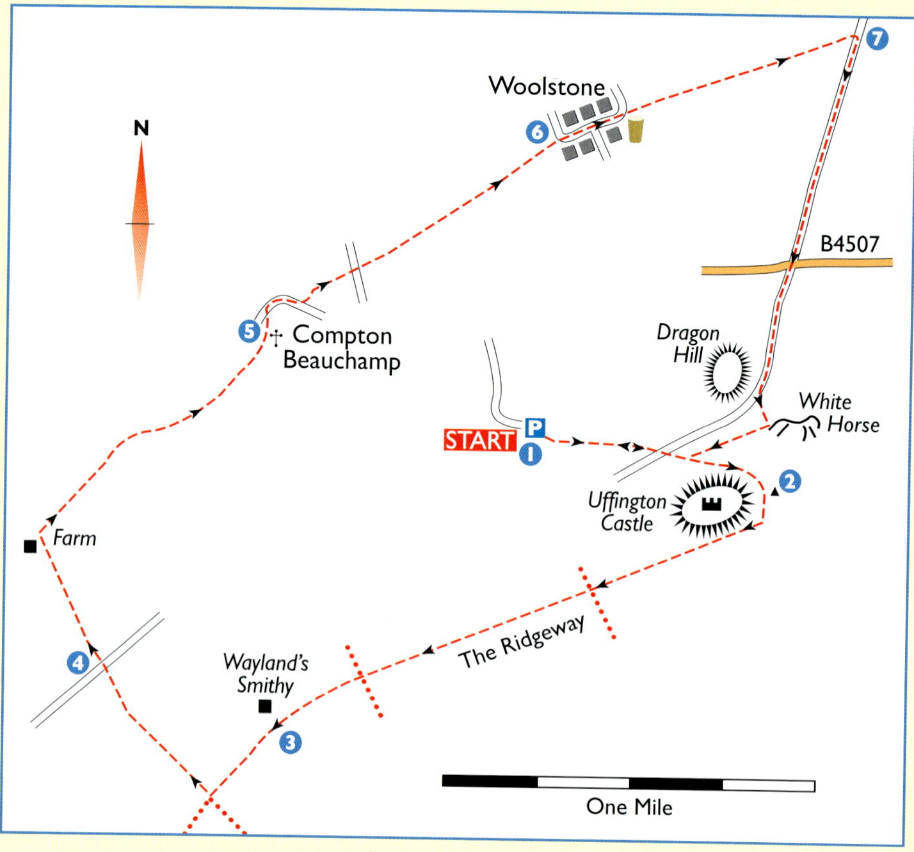

coalesced into loose confederations and petty kingdoms, headed by a ruling elite versed in the ways of war.

Modern-day Oxfordshire was divided between three tribes: the Catuvellauni in the east, the Atrebates in the south, and the Dobunni in the west and north. The Thames valley was a frontier between these confederations. Inter-tribal warfare was by no means endemic, and by and large these tribes peacefully co-existed, but the threat of violence was always there and they needed to have a defensive site to which the population could withdraw in times of emergency. Communities increasingly lived in the shadow of hillforts, which could offer protection. These forts in turn were built ever larger and grander, a visible symbol of the power and prestige of the local ruler.

One such hillfort was Uffington Castle, built by the Dobunni around AD 700. With its huge ramparts and dominating position, it was clearly designed to overawe potential enemies. Like the modern-day nuclear deterrent the important thing about hillforts in the Iron Age was their existence, not their use, for no tribal army of that day could reasonably hope to take such an impregnable obstacle by force.

THE WALK

1 Leave the car park from the top left-hand corner, up steps signposted 'Picnic area'. Pass through the picnic area and a second gate onto the open hillside and go half left over open ground towards the White Horse seen in the distance. Go through a gate and cross a minor road to ascend a clear chalk track opposite (signposted 'Bridleway'). At a cross-track in a few yards, do not turn left towards the White Horse but continue straight on up the path towards the skyline. Soon a triangulation point comes into view. About 50 yards short of the trig point turn right to enter Uffington Castle.

The Iron Age hillfort of Uffington Castle was built around 700 BC by the Dobunni tribe, who occupied the upper Thames and lower Severn valleys throughout the Iron Age. It is in a commanding hilltop position, 856 ft above sea level, with a single ditch and embankment built around the top of the hill and enclosing a site 8 acres in size. The banks would have been more precipitous than today and a strong wooden palisade would have faced downhill, giving further protection in times of trouble. There was only one entrance, to the west, on the opposite side of the fort to where you entered: all the other gaps through the encircling embankment have been made later.

In times of peace, the hillfort was an administrative and commercial centre for the tribe, and would have had huts for the regular inhabitants, stockades and temporary accommodation for passing traders. The bulk of the tribe lived in outlying farms in the countryside beyond. In times of war, the fort provided emergency shelter for the neighbourhood, and in the centre was plenty of open space to house the cattle of the surrounding farms.

Uffington Castle would have been virtually impregnable against attack by neighbouring tribes, who lacked the weapons to take the castle by siege and the discipline to storm its ramparts. However, the Roman legions possessed both discipline and siege artillery, and when the Dobunni resisted the Roman advance up the Thames valley in AD 45, Uffington Castle was besieged. After its fall, resistance to the invader collapsed and the Romans occupied the rest of the territory of the Dobunni without difficulty (see Walk 2).

It is very rewarding to circumnavigate Uffington Castle, as this gives a vivid impression of the size of the site. Immediately inside the entrance, turn left and climb up onto the embankment. Follow the embankment around in a clockwise direction until you return to the starting point.

Halfway around the embankment, on the western side, note the original entrance gate to the fort. The gate was always the weakest point of a hillfort defensively, and whereas the rest of the fort is surrounded by a single ditch and bank, the gate was protected by a second ditch and bank, which can still be clearly seen. The gate itself would have been a movable wooden structure, often a pile of logs, inside intricate earth ramparts that defended it.

2   To continue the walk, leave the castle by the entrance where you came in, turn right to pass the trig point and go straight on to a gate beside a signpost, leading onto the Ridgeway long-distance path.

The Ridgeway is one of the oldest roads in western Europe, running along the top of the chalk downs from the Bristol Channel to the Thames and enabling travellers to avoid the densely forested plains below. It was first used by man in the Old Stone Age, when the earliest hunter-gatherers followed great migrating herds of wild horses and cattle, seeking hides, horns and meat. By the New Stone Age it was becoming a major routeway for trade between scattered communities. Originally, it was a series of parallel tracks along the ridge of the Downs, with travellers taking the one most dry or convenient at the time. The present single track known as the Ridgeway follows this route, but was not defined in its present width or course until the 18th century.

Turn right along the broad and flinty track of the Ridgeway. After ½ mile go over a cross-track and continue straight on. After a further ½ mile, ignore a footpath pointing right and go straight on, and shortly after that, cross a partially metalled track and continue straight on.

3   In 400 yards, look for a footpath sign on the right, pointing to Wayland's Smithy.

There were two tombs or barrows constructed on this site, at widely different times. The first was built around 3500 BC. This type of tomb was known as a long barrow, an oval chamber dug out of the chalk, the interior lined with wood and the outside edged with stones. The barrow was in use over a considerable period, being opened at successive intervals as fresh corpses were interred. The remains of 15 people, of all ages and both sexes, were found inside. The communities who built the barrows were not settled in one place: they would move on every few decades once the land became exhausted. Consequently over time the barrows became further and further away from where the people now lived, and required longer and longer journeys to bury the dead in them. This may be the reason why the barrow was eventually permanently sealed and abandoned.

Around 1300 BC, a second tomb was built on top of the original one, much larger and rectangular in shape, 180 ft long and 46 ft wide. Within the burial mound were three stone-lined burial chambers, arranged in a cross shape and leading off an entrance hall. This tomb was used for several centuries before finally being sealed, and contained eight bodies.

The trees that surround the site today were not there when the mound was constructed, and the conspicuous burial mounds served another purpose. By the Middle Stone Age, man had ceased to be nomadic and had settled down to live by farming in a specific area. Burial mounds were placed on high airy places, possibly for religious reasons, but with the additional use as a territorial marker. Certainly by now communities were starting to become linked to specific geographic areas, and settlements with permanent territories were developing. It is possible that clearly visible tribal burial mounds were used to mark the boundaries of a community's territory.

The name Wayland's Smithy was given to the mound by the Saxons around 1100, who thought it was the home of one of their heroes, Wayland, Blacksmith to the Gods, seen locally as an incarnation of Odin himself, King of the Gods. Legend had it that any traveller who left a silver coin on the mound would have his horse shod by Wayland, with shoes that would never wear out.

Continue along the Ridgeway. After ¼ mile, at a cross-track, turn right onto a track signed 'Restricted Byway'. Follow the broad green track. Eventually the track, now chalky, starts to descend, soon becoming paved.

As you start your descent, look to your left. On the slopes of the dry valley are a complex series of ridges and platforms. These are strip lychetts, ancient agricultural land. The hillside was levelled into a series of terraces upon which crops could be grown. These lychetts date from the early Middle Ages, but were in all probability constructed on top of earlier platforming that was contemporary with Uffington Hillfort and Wayland's Smithy.

Follow the paved track down to the road.

4 Cross half left over the road and then follow a farm drive, signed 'Byway D'Arcy Dalton Way'. Ignore a turn to the left but keep straight on along a track, with a fence and the farmhouse to your left. At the end of the track keep ahead, converging with the fence on your left, and follow the fence down to a gate. Go through the gate, and immediately turn right across a stile beside a second gate.

Keep ahead along the top of a large field. At the far end cross stiles and a footbridge and keep straight on up the field. Keep ahead, the hedge close on your right hand. Pass into the next field and keep ahead, the hedge still on your right. Pass into the next field and keep ahead across the middle of the field to reach a kissing gate. Go through the gate and cross the next field, aiming for a gate in front of the church seen opposite. Pass through the gate and descend the right hand edge of the field, keeping the churchyard on your right.

5 At the bottom of the churchyard go through a gate onto the drive to the church. Turn left and follow the drive out to the road. Go straight along the road for 30 yards. Where the road bears right, keep straight on through a gate and up a track, but before doing so pause and look back.

Behind you is the gateway to Compton Beauchamp House, with the church of St Swithun beside it. Leading from the manor house, down the slope to your left, is a broad drive, now bordered by fences and hedges, which was once the main carriageway up to the house. Up the slope to your right is the tiny hamlet of Knighton. This scene is a superb microcosm of feudal life: the manor house with the church almost attached to it, the cottages of its retainers clustered out of sight but conveniently close by. In Saxon times Compton was a royal manor, owned by Edward the Confessor. In the 13th century the Beauchamp family, Earls of Warwick, acquired the manor just long enough to change its name, improve the house and build the church of St Swithin. The moated manor house was rebuilt in Tudor times, and a Georgian wing was subsequently added.

Continue forward along the track. Where the track bears right in front of a small building, bear left around the building, maintaining the same general direction along the right-hand edge of a field, with trees and a hedge on your right. Cross a stile into a second field and continue in the same direction, still with trees and hedge on your right, to emerge onto a road. Cross the road to a field gate opposite. Cross the stile to the left of the gate and continue the same line of advance, with a fence on your right. Keep ahead along two fields. At the end of the second field, go half-left to a stile and footbridge.

Cross the footbridge and 5 yards later turn left and then almost immediately turn right to cross a stile into a field. Continue along the right-hand edge of the field, with a hedge on your right, to a wooden gate.

There are fine views of Uffington Castle over the hedge on your right. Its commanding hilltop position, dominating the plain below, is clearly illustrated.

Go through the gate and keep straight on, along the right-hand edge of the field.

A view of the White Horse on the slope ahead and to your right, starts to open up. The White Horse has been described as 'a triumph of artistic omission': the carving itself is a very schematic representation of a horse, and it is the eye and the imagination that fills in the rest of the detail.

Pass under a power line to a stile. Cross the stile and continue ahead past the gate of a house onto a road.

6 Continue straight on down the road, past the entrance to Upper Farm, and soon passing the White Horse Inn on your right. Ignore a turning to your right and continue ahead through the village of Woolstone. Where the road turns left, continue ahead, over a stile and along the right-hand edge of two fields. Cross a stile and keep ahead through woodland into another field, now planted with young trees. Continue with the hedge on your left and eventually with fencing on your right.

7 Turn right along the lane for ½ mile to reach the B4507. Cross the road and ascend the minor road opposite. After 500 yards the road levels out at a cutting between Dragon Hill on the right and White Horse Hill on the left. You may wish to detour right up the steps onto Dragon Hill.

This chalk outcrop has been artificially levelled on its top, at a time and for a purpose never understood. Certainly it was done in prehistoric times, possibly for religious or strategic purposes. This is the spot where according to legend St George met and slew his dragon. The bare patch of earth is reputedly caused by the dragon's acid blood, and the White Horse on the hillside above is claimed to represent George's steed. It is interesting that the legend of St George picks up upon several mythical themes that have passed down through local legend over the ages. The neighbourhood is dominated by the enigmatic White Horse, carved in the late Bronze Age at a time when the horse cult was predominant, and society was increasingly dominated by a horse-riding aristocracy. Much later, in Saxon times, the Norse god Odin was a mighty horse-riding warrior and the focus of a horse cult. Wayland was an incarnation of Odin, and dragon-slaying played a significant part in Norse legends. Thus the area had a tradition of legends regarding horse-riding warriors and dragon slaying. It is possible that a story of the Christian hero-saint was superimposed upon existing pagan legends already associated with the area.

Return to the road. From the road go left up a clear path to reach the White Horse. Take care not to walk upon the Horse itself, which is subject to continual erosion by careless tourists. If possible, contour around a little to the left.

This White Horse is the oldest chalk figure in the country. Popular tradition says it is of Saxon origin and was carved to commemorate King Alfred's victory at the battle of Ashdown in AD 871. In reality its origins are far older, and it is probable that the Horse is over 3,000 years old. Its shape resembles horses depicted on Iron Age coins, and it most likely dates from the late Bronze Age or early Iron Age. Why White Horses were carved on hillsides throughout this part of Britain is uncertain, but may have reflected a change in social/religious circumstances. Certainly this was a period when the use of the horse, both for agriculture and for warfare, was becoming more widespread, and society was becoming dominated by a horse-borne warrior elite.

The Horse was created by 10 ft wide trenches being cut 2 or 3 ft deep into the required shape and then refilled with white chalk. The horse is 365 ft long. It is still in the same position in which it was originally dug, although is now somewhat thinner than originally. It has been recut and the trenches rewhitened with chalk over the centuries, and one such cleaning operation is the probable origin of the Alfred story.

From the top of the White Horse, turn right, keeping the drop to your right, and follow the clear track that contours around the slope. At a cross-track, turn right and descend to a minor road. Cross the road and go through a gate opposite. Retrace your outward steps along a clear path across the hillside back to the car park.

NORTH LEIGH:
THE ROMANS INVADE

Length: 3 miles

The remains of the Roman villa at North Leigh

HOW TO GET THERE: The walk starts from the village green at Combe, which is on a network of minor roads, 1 mile north of the A4095 at Long Hanborough, and 2 miles south of the B4437 Charlbury to Wootton road.

PARKING: There is ample parking around the village green.

MAP: OS Landranger 164 (GR 413159).

INTRODUCTION

A short walk through peaceful and attractive countryside, mainly using field paths and crossing the river Evenlode, to visit the Roman villa at North Leigh. Route-finding is easy, and there is only the occasional gentle incline.

HISTORICAL BACKGROUND

The area of modern-day Oxfordshire was already well settled by British tribes when the Romans arrived, and it was brought under control rapidly and relatively peacefully. The Thames valley was subdued within four years of the Romans landing in Kent in AD 43, and, after Uffington Castle had fallen (see Walk 1) both the Dobunni to the south-west and the Catuvellauni to the east accepted Roman rule with little further resistance. How much the occupation was initially resented by the existing British population is unknown, but part of the Roman genius was in getting an occupied race to accept the benefits of their civilisation and thus fight to preserve it. The Romans had no prejudice against race or colour, and easily assimilated local populations into the Empire.

The valleys of the Evenlode and the Glyme had rich arable soil, easy access to pastures for sheep on the surrounding slopes, and fuel and game in nearby Wychwood Forest. Consequently they were already dotted with pre-Roman settlements, which usually took the form of a farmhouse or villa, home to the owner, in the centre of a hamlet within which the retainers and the livestock were housed. These owners were not usurped by incoming Romans, but instead were absorbed into an increasingly Romanised society. They prospered under the occupation, benefiting from security, good communications and a buoyant economy created by increased markets. This prosperity was reflected in the richer and better designed houses, the rich jewellery and other goods, and a more civilised lifestyle.

A number of Roman villas have been excavated in the Evenlode valley, of

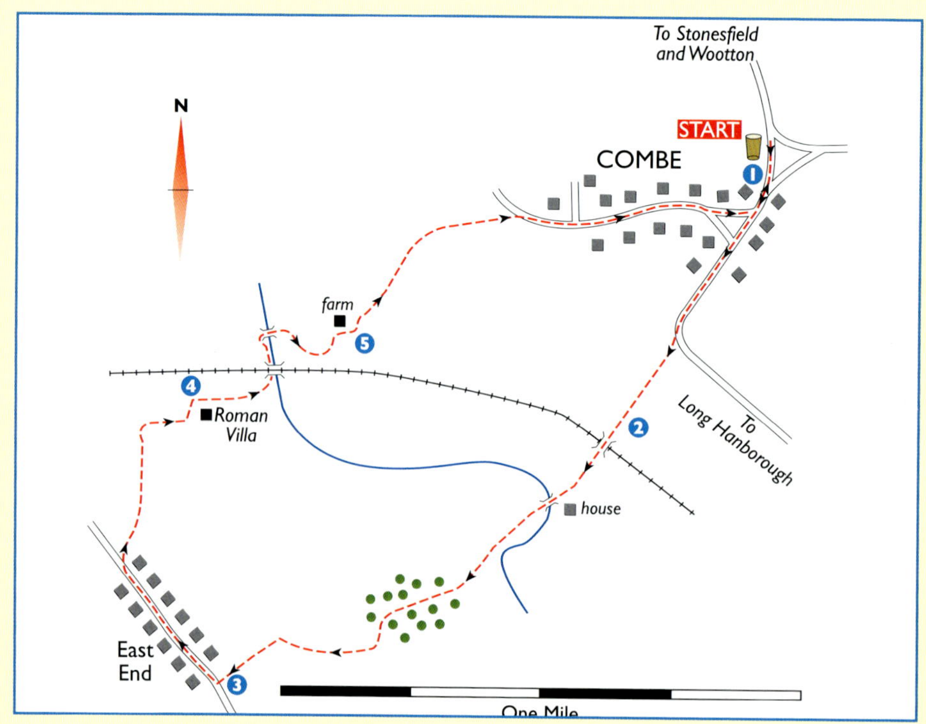

which North Leigh is the most complete. It was not owned by 'Romans', that is, settlers from the Empire, but by native Britons – one of the noble families of the Dobunni who had a seat on the tribal council and a town house in the capital Corinium (Cirencester). They were part of the governing class who ruled the Roman province of Britain, and who incorporated the luxuries and amenities that the Romans had introduced into their everyday life.

THE WALK

1 With your back to the Cock Inn, turn right along the village green. Follow the road around to the right, signed 'Long Hanborough'. Pass 'The Old Chapel' on the left and ignore two turns to the right. In 250 yards, where the road turns sharp left, keep ahead along a track, signed 'Footpath North Leigh'.

2 Follow the track over a railway and keep ahead, soon descending. In 80 yards, before a gate to a house, turn right off the track and follow a footpath steeply down through trees. Cross a footbridge and go half left across a field, towards the river bank ahead. On reaching the river continue in your same direction, leaving the river and heading for a gate into woods ahead. Cross a stile and footbridge. Ignore a green track to the right but keep left on a footpath through trees. Cross a second footbridge and keep ahead along the footpath. Ascend gradually and swing left to reach a waymark post, where turn right down through the trees to cross a footbridge.

Follow the path out to a field and keep ahead, a hedge on your left hand. On reaching a gravelled track keep ahead, hedge and house on your right. In 50 yards, turn left with the track and follow it past houses. Ignore side turns and keep ahead to reach a road.

3 Turn right along the road and follow it through the village of East End. At the end of the village, turn right down a track, signed 'Access only to Roman villa'. Follow the track for ¼ mile.

There are good views of North Leigh Roman villa below on your right.

Turn right down a side track to reach the villa.

There had been a farmstead on this site for many years before the Roman invasion. Once it was part of the Roman Empire, the economic prosperity of the area increased dramatically, and with it the wealth of the local gentry. The first Roman-style buildings at North Leigh were constructed late in the 1st century AD. Although added to and altered over succeeding centuries, the shape remained much as can be seen today. The villa was constructed in a square around a central courtyard: on three sides were ranges of one-storey buildings containing nearly 60 rooms for living, sleeping and entertaining, including two bath-houses. As well as internal doors, each room opened onto a covered colonnaded walkway which ran around all three sides of the court. The fourth side was a wall, pierced by the gateway leading from the court to the drive, which in turn connected to the road leading to Akeman Street, a mile away. All rooms had underfloor heating, the ducts of which can been seen today, and most had elaborate mosaic floors, part of which have been excavated and can be seen in the covered building on the site.

Although the first Romanised buildings were constructed before AD 100, the villa did not reach its final form until the end of the 4th century. It continued to be occupied after the Romans left Britain in AD 410, by a thoroughly Romanised elite who maintained Roman values for some years more. In the final stages of its existence the villa had ceased to be lived in by its owners, who had probably moved into the security of one of the nearby cities in the face of an increasingly unruly country. The villa was finally gutted by fire, whether deliberate or accidental is not known, and abandoned.

The mosaics can be viewed at any time through a window, but are only open to visitors one day a month April-September, for a small admission charge, free to English Heritage members. The villa itself is open any reasonable time, admission free.

4   To continue the walk, go through a kissing gate to the left of the entrance to the villa and immediately turn right along the side of a field. In the field corner cross a footbridge, go through a kissing gate and then keep ahead across the field to a railway arch seen on the far side. Turn left under the railway arch, the river Evenlode on your right. Cross a stile and keep ahead, the river still on your right.

Just a mile north of here, ahead of you, was the Roman road of Akeman Street, connecting Cirencester with St Albans, the capitals of the neighbouring British tribes the Dodunni and the Catuvellauni. A spur from that road ran via a ford through the Evenlode, to North Leigh villa.

In 100 yards turn right over a bridge and then turn right again, following a track to a gate into a field. Follow the clear track up and left to reach a farm.

5   Cross a stile and turn right. Follow the drive, the farmhouse on your left and cattle sheds on your right. At the end of the farm bear left with the drive and continue along the tarmac drive between fields. Follow this track as it winds through trees and climbs to the village of Combe. Keep ahead and follow the lane. Ignore Chatterpie Lane on your left but keep ahead to a fork in the lane. Bear left to the main road and turn left back to the village green.

REFRESHMENTS

The Cock Inn at Combe offers a good range of beers and food in a pleasant atmosphere. It has a beer garden, benches overlooking the village green, and a separate dining area. Telephone: 01993 891288.

WALK 3

DORCHESTER AND THE RETURN OF CHRISTIANITY

Length: 5 miles

The Iron Age ramparts of Dyke Hills

HOW TO GET THERE: Dorchester is just south of the A415, 7 miles east of Abingdon.

PARKING: The walk starts from the Bridge End (free) car park, at the southern end of Dorchester High Street.

MAP: OS Landranger 164 (GR 579939).

INTRODUCTION

From the water meadows of the rivers Thame and Thames, this walk climbs to Castle Hill, with its splendid views across the Thames plain, before returning via the enigmatic Dyke Hills to historic Dorchester and its ancient Abbey church.

HISTORICAL BACKGROUND

Dorchester was witness to the struggle to reintroduce Christianity into England after the departure of the Romans. Christianity had been imposed upon the Roman Empire by the Emperor Constantine in the 4th century AD. A Christian Romano-British culture continued in Britain for many years after the withdrawal of the Roman legions in AD 410, but it was gradually swamped by the steady influx of Germanic tribes, who brought their own religious beliefs and their own

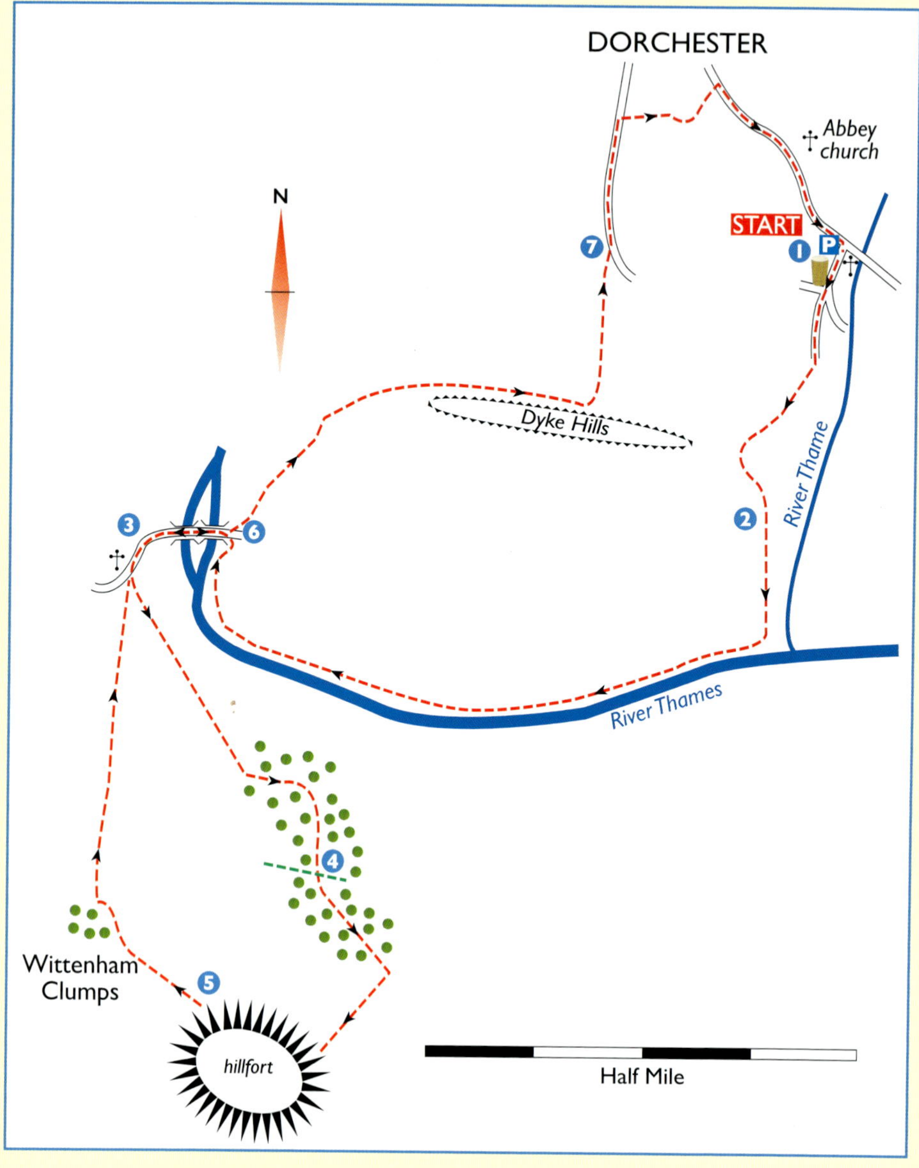

social organisation. With these 'Saxon' immigrants, Britain gradually reverted to a rural-based tribal society, with political control in the hands of a local landowning aristocracy. This fragmented social organisation, based around many small kingdoms, led to frequent border disputes, with the constant danger of unrest and outright warfare. Christianity started to re-emerge in Britain from the end of the 6th century onwards, and missionaries were soon converting local kings, and through them their subjects, back to the Christian faith. The rigid hierarchy of the Church, with its division into bishoprics, influenced and was influenced by, the emerging political map of Britain.

In AD 635 King Oswald of Northumbria, overlord of the Saxon kingdoms and a Christian, met King Cynegils, the pagan king of Wessex, at the town of Dorcic (later called Dorchester) in Wessex, to make a lasting peace between the two kingdoms. To seal this, Oswald married Cynegils' daughter, and Cynegils was baptised as a Christian by Bishop Birinus, who had accompanied Oswald southwards. Birinus was given Dorchester as his Episcopal See, the centre of his bishopric, and a cathedral was built there. In AD 660 the Northumbrian-Wessex alliance went to war with Mercia, during which conflict King Oswald was killed. The resulting political instability led to the See being moved to Winchester, and Dorchester became part of the diocese of Mercian Leicester, to be ruled by secular canons.

The Danish invasion of West Mercia destroyed Leicester, and in AD 869 Dorchester was re-established as the seat of an expanded bishopric, stretching from the Thames valley to the Humber. For the next 200 years, Dorchester was one of the most important and powerful Saxon bishoprics, until the Norman Conquest swept away the Saxon structure of government, both secular and ecclesiastical. The first and only Norman bishop of Dorchester, Remigius, relocated his See, his administrative and ecclesiastic capital, to Lincoln in 1070, and Dorchester dropped out of history.

THE WALK

❶ Walk down Bridge End, away from the bridge and the main road, passing public conveniences. You soon pass the Roman Catholic church of St Birinus on your left, to reach the (now closed) Chequers Inn. Immediately past the Chequers, do not keep ahead towards the green but instead fork half right along the gravelled Wittenham Lane, just to the right of a post box. At the end of the houses, do not continue along the track but go through the gate ahead, to the right of the track, and follow a clear path along the left-hand side of the field. At the end of the field, go through a kissing gate and keep ahead for 10 yards to a pillbox on the left.

The Iron Age ramparts of Dyke Hills are to your right. You will see these more closely at the end of the walk.

Do not enter the field containing the pillbox but bear left, keeping the hedge and fence to your left.

2 Go through a kissing gate in the fence ahead and keep straight on, parallel to the river Thame on your left hand, to reach the banks of the river Thames, at the end of a footbridge. Turn right along the river bank, with the river on your left hand. Leave the meadow by a kissing gate and continue along a footpath along the side of the river. Leave the footpath by a gate and follow the river bank around two sides of a field to a bridge. Pass underneath and immediately turn right to get onto the bridge. Cross the river.

3 Follow the track over a second bridge and up to the church of St Peter at Little Wittenham. Opposite the end of the church turn left through a squeeze stile, signed 'Bridleway to Shillingford Bridge 2m'. Do not follow the clear path ahead, alongside a hedge, but go half left, signed 'Little Wittenham Wood', following a path across a meadow with the river initially down on your left, to a gate, leading into woods. Follow the broad track through the woods for 100 yards, then turn right and take a clear path up through trees. The path soon levels out. In a short distance, at a fork, keep right and maintain your line of advance.

4 Soon you reach a T-junction with a track. Turn left down the track, first descending but soon climbing. Ignore a side turning to the right, but 50 yards later turn right at a T-junction, to a gateway leading into a huge field. Turn right along a path following the edge of the field, with the woods on your right hand.

Brightwell barrow can be seen in the distance on your left, on top of a hill and itself topped with a clump of trees. This is a Neolithic burial mound, and its conspicuous airy site was chosen not only for religious reasons but also for territorial ones: the presence of the tomb announced the long-term connection between a people and an area of land, a visual reminder of who owned the land both to the community and its neighbours (see Wayland's Smithy, Walk 1).

Ignore a gate on the right and keep on up the field, climbing steadily with the woods on your right. At the top of the slope, follow a path through bushes to a gate leading into the hillfort.

The hillfort on Castle Hill was constructed during the early Iron Age by the Catuvellauni tribe. These people were farmers, who grazed their herds of sheep, goats and cattle on the upland pastures around here and practised arable farming on the fertile plain. Hillforts were not permanently occupied: the community lived in scattered farmsteads in the fields below. The forts were constructed to provide temporary shelter for the community and its livestock in times of emergency, and also to act as centres for trade and administration. This hillfort was later abandoned when the community made a permanent settlement on the site of present-day Dorchester, protected by the ramparts of the Dyke Hills.

Climb over the outer rampart and through the ditch to reach the open grassy centre of the fort. It is worthwhile turning left and walking around the summit, to appreciate both the commanding position of the fort, the magnificent views from it, and the extent of the ramparts surrounding the fort. Eventually get to the far side of the grassy centre of the hillfort, either by walking around the perimeter or by following a path through the clump of trees in the fort's centre. Either way you need to reach the top of a flight of wooden steps, opposite a conspicuous stand of trees known as 'Wittenham Clumps'.

5 Descend the steps into the ditch and up the far rampart to a gate. Cross a track, with a metal field gate on your right. Go through a gate straight ahead and follow a broad path up the hill to Wittenham Clumps. Circle right around the trees, with views down over Dorchester, until you reach a seat and a disused plinth. Here turn right and go downhill, aiming straight at the church seen at the bottom of the hill. At the bottom of the slope go through a gate and keep straight on, with the hedge on your left hand. Go through the gate opposite St Peter's again, and turn right down the lane back to the bridge over the river. Cross the bridge.

6 At the far side of the bridge go half left across the field, aiming for a gate more or less in line with the Abbey church seen ahead. Go through the gate and keep ahead along an enclosed footpath. At the end of the footpath keep ahead, with the Dyke Hills on your right.

The Dyke Hills were raised in the Iron Age. The Catuvellauni tribe occupied much of the land to the north and west of present-day London. Under the greatest of their kings, Cunobelinus (the model for Shakespeare's Cymbeline) their territories encompassed all of modern Hertfordshire, the western side of Essex and Suffolk, and most of Northamptonshire and Oxfordshire. The Catuvellauni built a town here upon the banks of the Thames, both to grow crops on the fertile river plain and also for fishing. To protect their town they surrounded it with a huge double rampart, with two ditches, one between the ramparts and the other around the outside. The rampart surrounded most of present-day Dorchester.

This fortification is unusual on two counts: firstly, it was on a lowland plain not on a hilltop; secondly, it surrounded a permanently occupied town and was not intended for use only in emergencies, as were many Iron Age hillforts (see Walk 1). Both factors speak of the importance of the site to the Catuvellauni. It is also unusual to find lowland Iron Age fortifications still visible: most have long since been built over.

Dorchester Abbey church

Approximately halfway along the dyke, where the embankment bends slightly right, look for a yellow post in the fence on your right. Here turn left on a path across the field, leading towards houses. Follow the path out to a lane and turn left.

7   Go along the lane for 350 yards. Just past a white, thatched house, turn right down an alley to the right of the gate of No 19. Follow the alley past houses and a terrace of thatched cottages, and then bear left to reach the High Street, opposite the White Hart.

Dorchester was once a staging post on the turnpike to London and the High Street has a number of inns that owe their origins to this. The turnpike was a privately owned toll road, maintained to a high standard to enable the fast passage of coaches.

Turn right down the High Street. In 200 yards, where the road curves right at the George Hotel, is a lychgate on the left, leading to the Abbey.

After Bishop Birinus had baptised King Cynegils of Wessex in AD 635, he was given Dorcic (Dorchester) as his Episcopal See, and promptly set about building and dedicating a cathedral in the town. The present Dorchester Abbey stands on the site of that original

Saxon cathedral. Birinus, later sainted, died in AD 650 and was buried in Dorchester cathedral, although ten years later the threat of war with the neighbouring kingdom of Mercia led to the See, and Birinus' remains, being moved to Winchester for safety. The cathedral was re-established as the bishops' seat in AD 869 and remained so until 1067, when the Norman conquest moved the See to Lincoln.

REFRESHMENTS

The Fleur de Lys pub in Dorchester has a good range of beers and the most reasonably priced menu of the three pubs in the town. It has oak-panelled bars and a large beer garden. Telephone: 01865 340502.

Nothing now remains of the original Saxon cathedral. In 1140 it was refounded as part of the Augustinian abbey of Dorchester, and a splendid new church built in the Norman style. The tomb of St Birinus was opened in 1225, and the abbey became a popular place of pilgrimage, becoming very rich as a result. This wealth was used in part for extensive rebuilding and extension over the next two centuries. Under the religious reforms of Henry VIII's reign, the abbey was dissolved in 1536 and the shrine of St Birinus destroyed. The land and buildings were bought by Richard Beauforest, a local landowner, who continued the demolition of the Abbey started by the king's commissioners, reusing the building materials elsewhere. The church however was left, as a place of worship for the local people, and has remained the parish church of Dorchester ever since.

Today, all that remains of the former abbey is the church of St Peter and St Paul, the former Guest House, now used as a grammar school and museum, and the cloister garden to the rear of the building. The church itself is a splendid example of 13th- and 14th-century architecture. Especially noteworthy are the People's Chapel, with its fine medieval wall paintings, and a lead Norman font, one of the finest in England. The Jesse window, with stone branches and 14th-century stained glass, traces Christ's descent from Jesse and is a beautiful example of a Norman church window. There is also a modern shrine to St Birinus.

After visiting the Abbey, continue along the High Street for 100 yards, curving left with the road to return to the car park.

WALK 4

WALLINGFORD: THE NORMANS IN OXFORDSHIRE

Length: 5½ miles

The majestic medieval bridge at Wallingford

HOW TO GET THERE:
Wallingford is 10 miles south of Oxford on the A4130 and the A4074.

PARKING: The walk starts at the pay and display car park at the eastern, non-town end of Wallingford bridge, best approached from the A4074 by-pass.

MAP: OS Landranger 175 (GR 611894).

INTRODUCTION

The walk follows the bank of the river Thames past the oldest church in Wallingford and then uses pleasant rural paths and tracks to return to the historic town and an exploration of the remains of its castle.

HISTORICAL BACKGROUND

Wallingford commands a crossing of the river Thames, and as such it was important strategically to the Normans. When William the Conqueror defeated the army of King Harold at Hastings in 1066, this did not mean an automatic victory, for the Saxon earls were not prepared to submit to the Norman usurper. William cautiously advanced upon the Saxon capital London by a very indirect route, swinging up to the Thames and following the south bank of the river, then passing London by, to cross the Thames at Wallingford and attack London from the west.

William left one of his lieutenants, Robert D'Oyley, to secure the strategically important Wallingford, and between 1067 and 1071 D'Oyley built a strong castle on the king's behalf, to command the river crossing. The town expanded rapidly under the Normans. It was important enough to have its own mint, and received its royal charter from Henry II in 1155, making it the oldest royal borough in England. The castle remained a royal possession, and was expanded twice, firstly by King John and later in the reign of John's son Henry III, whose brother Richard, Earl of Cornwall was constable of the castle.

Wallingford played a leading role in the civil war between Stephen (nominated as heir to Henry II) and his cousin Matilda, Henry II's daughter (who also claimed the throne). It was Matilda's main stronghold, commanding the Thames valley and threatening London, and Stephen made three unsuccessful attempts to take the town. The final peace treaty between Stephen and Matilda was signed at Wallingford in 1153. In 1307 the castle was given by Edward II to his favourite, Piers Gaveston, who was created Baron Wallingford. In 1327 the castle became the headquarters of the conspiracy between Edward's queen, Isabella, and her lover Roger Mortimer, to overthrow King Edward, and later still Edward III

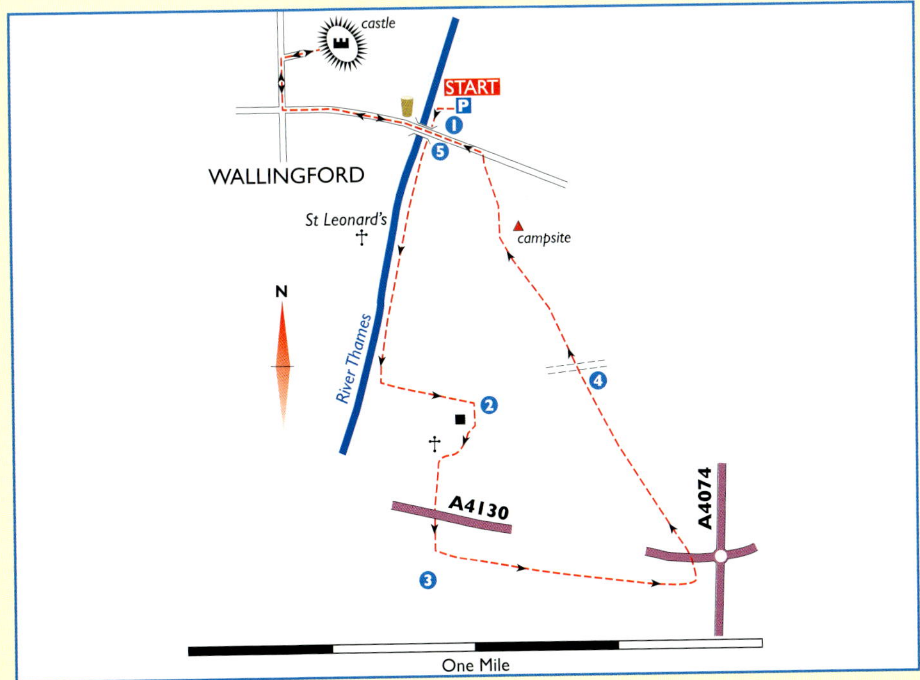

besieged the castle in 1330 to capture and execute Mortimer in revenge for his father's murder.

Although over the next 300 years Wallingford Castle had many famous residents, it did not see significant action again until the Civil War, when it was fortified by the Royalists to defend the approaches to their capital, Oxford. In 1646 it withstood siege for 16 weeks before surrendering to Parliamentary forces. It was briefly used as a prison, but in 1652 Cromwell ordered the castle razed to prevent its use ever again as a stronghold.

THE WALK

❶ Cross the car park to the banks of the river Thames and turn left, passing under Wallingford bridge.

There has been a Thames crossing at this point since prehistoric times. The first bridge here was Roman. The predecessor of the present bridge was built in the 14th century, and although it has been rebuilt many times, the structure has remained largely unaltered. It is 900 ft long, only 15 ft shorter than the old London Bridge, and one of the longest medieval bridges built in England. In Tudor times it was renovated, using stone from neighbouring religious houses. During the Civil War some of its 19 arches were demolished and replaced with drawbridges, to facilitate its defence. The present bridge was built in 1809.

Follow the river bank, passing St Leonard's church on the opposite bank after 400 yards.

St Leonard's is the oldest existing church in Wallingford. It dates originally from Saxon times, and although much of the original Saxon building was rebuilt in the Norman style after the Conquest, some Saxon herringbone stonework can still be seen. The church was used as a barracks by Parliamentarian troops during the Civil War, and suffered considerable damage. It was extensively reconstructed in Victorian times.

Continue along the river bank, passing through a gate and walking on until opposite a modern, balconied clubhouse on the far bank. Turn left and walk across the meadow, directly away from the river bank. Pass to the right of a large tree in mid-field and aim to the left of barns on the opposite side of the field.

❷ At the far side of the field, turn right along the fence to a metal kissing gate, beside a field gate and to the left of a barn. Go through the gate and keep straight on for 30 yards to reach a concrete farm drive. Keep straight on along the drive for further 20 yards, to a stile on the left, just before the gate into the farmyard. Cross the stile and maintain your direction down the drive, passing barns and the entrance to Newnham Farm House and Cottage on your right.

Soon you will pass Newnham Murren church on the right.

Newnham Murren church is Norman in origin. That it was built in more turbulent times is reflected by a peephole, which enabled occupants to privately study potential visitors before allowing them into the church.

Keep straight on along a tree-lined footpath. Where the footpath joins a paved footpath, keep straight on. The footpath soon becomes unsurfaced again and passes under the A4130. In 20 yards after the underpass, at a fingerpost at the top of a small rise, turn sharp left.

3 Follow the hedge-lined path, with the road off to your left. Go through a kissing gate and continue along the tree-lined path, ignoring a side turn to the right, and soon veering away from the road. Some 10 yards before a kissing gate leading out onto a busy road, turn left onto a narrow footpath at a fingerpost. Follow the footpath out to a road and cross to a finger post on the far side. Descend steps to a stile into a large field. Go half left across the field. At a white post on the far side, go through a gap in the hedge. Maintain your line of advance across the next field, to a stile half-right across the corner of the field.

4 Go through a gap in the hedge onto a farm drive. Turn right and almost immediately turn left along an enclosed footpath between fields. Follow the footpath for 600 yards, keeping straight on at a cross-track and following the side of a camp site. At a T-junction, turn right along the track to reach the main road. Turn left back to Wallingford bridge and the car park.

5 To visit Wallingford castle, cross the bridge and keep ahead along the High Street. The castle is now a public park and open daily from dawn to dusk.

The Thames can be crossed easily at Wallingford, which has been of strategic importance since the Iron Age. The ancient British settlement here was replaced in the first century AD by a Roman town, astride the main road from London to Cirencester. After the Romans left England, Wallingford survived as a Romano-British town, whose inhabitants were eventually absorbed into the encroaching Saxon invaders. Wallingford became an important Saxon burgh, and the Saxon street plan is still discernible. The town was fortified by Alfred the Great in AD 886, part of his front line defences against the Danes. The open area called the Bullscroft, now a public playing field, is surrounded on two sides by the embankments built by Alfred. After the fragile peace negotiated by Alfred collapsed, Wallingford was largely destroyed by the Danes in 1006.

Pass through traffic lights, and at the crossroads shortly after, turn right into Castle Street. Go along Castle Street for 50 yards, and then turn right down the drive to the George Inn. Where the drive turns right into the George, turn left through an archway into Castle Gardens.

Although little of the stone structure of Wallingford castle remains, the foundations and earthen embankments are still clearly visible. Today they are incorporated into the Castle Gardens, and a walk around these grounds gives a vivid impression of this once mighty castle.

The original castle was a typical Norman motte and bailey. An earth mound or motte was raised, and a palisaded keep built on top of it. A curtain wall was built around an area at the foot of the mound, creating an enclosed and defensible courtyard or bailey, in which wooden buildings would soon accumulate. Construction of Wallingford castle started in 1067 and a strong motte and bailey was completed by 1071. The castle was later extended twice. In the first decade of the 13th century a moat was dug around the southern, townside, foot of the motte, and an extra curtain wall built around three sides of the castle, creating a second (middle) bailey. In the period 1250-1270 a third curtain wall was built outside the second wall, creating a narrow, trenchlike outer bailey which acted as a dry moat around the castle.

The archway through which you enter the Castle Gardens passes through the line of the third, outer wall of the castle. You are standing in the outer bailey, and in front of you is a massive bank upon the top of which was the middle curtain wall.

Ascend the steps through the wall to enter the middle bailey. The mound of the motte, now tree-covered, is in front of you. As you walk towards this you are crossing the middle bailey, which was crowded with the wooden buildings that serviced the castle. A modern plank bridge crosses the line of the moat built to defend the approaches to the motte and inner bailey. Although technically dry, this moat is even today boggy and subject to flooding, and in the 13th century this would have been another defensive obstacle.

Climb to the top of the motte. There was a strong stone keep built on top of this mound, the ultimate line of defence for the castle. From the top of the mound you can trace the line of the inner bailey wall, the curtain wall of the original castle, which surrounds the inner bailey, north of the motte. A fragment of this curtain wall can still be seen. The land between the castle and the river was originally very marshy and almost impassable, adding a further line of defence to the castle on this side.

After viewing the castle, retrace your steps to Wallingford bridge. Cross the bridge using the pavement on the left-hand side, to reach steps leading down into the car park.

WINDSOR CASTLE: FROM NORMAN STRONGHOLD TO VICTORIAN PALACE

Length: 3½ miles

The castle dates back to 1070

HOW TO GET THERE: Windsor lies just off the M4 (Junction 6). The walk starts from the pedestrianised bridge that links Windsor and Eton. The bridge can be easily found from anywhere in the town.

PARKING: There is plenty of parking within Windsor, much of it pay-and-display.

MAP: OS Landranger 175 (GR 968772).

INTRODUCTION

From the vibrant and historic town of Eton, the route passes Eton College and its famous playing fields, then crosses fields to return along the banks of the river Thames to Windsor, with fine views of the castle. Today it is Britain's greatest royal fortress but this is the story of its journey from wooden fort to palace. Route-finding is easy, the terrain is flat and easy underfoot.

HISTORICAL BACKGROUND

When the Normans conquered England there was nothing at Windsor. Edward the Confessor had built a hunting lodge at Old Windsor, 3 miles away, and a small village had grown up around that, but Windsor itself was just an empty river valley. It did, however, have a strategically important position, with a steep chalk hill at a point where the Thames narrowed. In 1070 William the Conqueror erected a wooden fort on top of an artificial earthen mound, itself on top of the river cliff and surrounded by a wooden palisade. For a century Windsor Castle remained this basic structure, an isolated outpost commanding the Thames and the western approach to London.

William's great-grandson, Henry II, greatly improved the defences at Windsor. The wooden fort was replaced by the great stone keep, the Round Tower. Three enclosed courtyards or baileys were built around the keep, each surrounded by a strong curtain wall and enclosing the whole top of the hill, an area of over 13 acres. Henry's grandson, Henry III, further increased the defences, adding the high western wall that faced the growing town of Windsor, and including

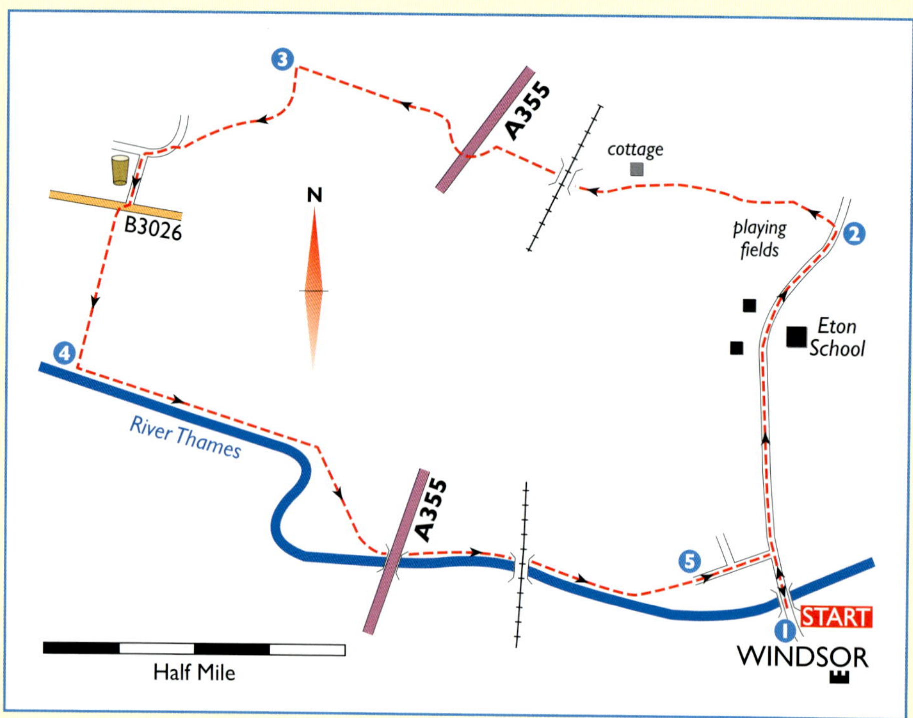

flanking towers. Windsor was now one of the strongest castles in England. Surrounded as it was with Windsor Great Park, it was especially favoured for hunting, and increasingly used as a royal residence.

By Tudor times the need for fortified castles was over. Henry VII and Henry VIII converted many of the buildings into palatial apartments and Elizabeth I added a terrace to the north, which gave access to the Great Park without going through the royal apartments. Seventy years later the State Apartments were rebuilt and modernized by Charles II. Through much of the 18th century Windsor was neglected, but George III, George IV and Queen Victoria all used it as their premier royal residence, and each of them modernised and added to it. The castle we see today is largely the result of those modernisations. The Round Tower was heightened considerably, as were a number of the towers on the curtain wall, and additional towers were built.

Today Windsor Castle is still used as a royal residence. William the Conqueror's simple fort has evolved beyond recognition into one of England's greatest castles.

THE WALK

1 Standing on the bridge connecting Windsor to Eton, with the castle behind you, walk ahead along the road, passing the George Inn on your left. Keep ahead along Eton High Street.

There was no settlement in Windsor or Eton before the castle was built in 1070. The first town started during the reign of Henry I and grew quickly. In 1277 it was made into a borough. The original town was on the southern bank of the Thames, below the castle walls, but soon spread onto this, the northern bank, where the tiny hamlet of Eton came into existence. It was the advent of the college in the 15th century that stimulated Eton's growth. This road, Eton High Street, is mainly 18th-century, and is lined with old pubs and buildings, many of which are today part of the service industry supporting Eton College.

Follow the road to pass between the buildings of Eton College, with the chapel and old school on your right and the buildings of the Lower School on the left.

Eton College was founded in 1440 by the pious King Henry VI (the same year that he also founded King's College, Cambridge) as a chantry chapel, with a school and almshouse attached. The school was to consist of 70 scholars, chosen for their intellectual ability, who would have most of their expenses paid and live free in the school. King Henry took a great personal interest in the building of Eton College, and the plans became ever more ambitious. The chapel, dining hall and cloisters are part of Henry's original building, although the chapel is only half the size the king intended: his deposition in 1461 halted the building work and for a while the very future of the college was in doubt. In 1463 Edward IV secured an edict from the Pope which allowed

Eton College to be annexed to St George's Chapel in Windsor Castle, as a prelude to closing the college down. The college provost however, succeeded in getting the edict revoked in 1467, thereby preserving the college's existence.

With the end of the Wars of the Roses work continued on Eton College. The Lower School buildings were finally completed at the end of the 15th century, and the imposing gatehouse known as Lupton's Tower was added in 1520. By this time the school was firmly established, and has continued as one of England's pre-eminent public schools to this day.

Eton is open for visits from Easter until the end of September, but visiting hours are variable, dependent upon school activities. There is an admission charge.

Bear right with the main road, passing the main college buildings on your right. Continue along the road to cross a bridge.

Look back right for fine views of the college.

2   About 100 yards past the bridge, turn left through a wooden gate at a footpath sign. The path crosses the end of the rugby pitch to a bridge and waymark sign 80 yards ahead.

You are crossing the playing fields attached to Eton College. According to Victorian mythology 'the battle of Waterloo was won upon the playing fields of Eton', a reference to the huge number of military, political and diplomatic leaders of the emerging British Empire who had been educated at Eton.

Cross the bridge and keep ahead along a gravelled path. Pass through a barrier to leave the grounds and keep ahead along a drive, passing Swimming Pool Cottages on your right. At a junction just past the houses, fork right at a footpath sign, and 15 yards later fork left, in front of gates to the golf course. Follow the drive under a railway arch and then keep ahead along a grassy track. At the road embankment, turn left with the track and follow it under the road, then zigzag with the track to resume your former direction. Follow the track, the meadow known as 'Common Ditch' on your left and a field on the right. At the far end of the field, at a fingerpost, turn left over a stile.

3   Keep ahead across the end of the meadow. Cross a footbridge and stile, and turn right. Follow the ditch on your right around to a gate leading into a lane. Turn left along the lane and follow it to the Greyhound pub. Turn left in front of the pub and follow the side street out to the main road. Cross the road and keep ahead along the tarmac cycle track opposite. Keep ahead at a cross-track and follow the tarmac track to reach the river.

4 Turn left and follow the path along the side of the Thames, the river on your right.

Look out for a concrete quay on the riverside, with a commemorative stone. This quay was a bathing place for Eton students, who were quaintly forbidden to land on the opposite bank. The quay was donated in memory of a student of the school, John Baker, a fine swimmer, who died in a flying accident in 1917.

Follow the path, the river always on your right, to go beneath first a road bridge and then a railway bridge. Windsor Castle comes into sight ahead.

The commanding hilltop position of Windsor Castle, dominating the Thames valley below, can clearly be seen from here. During its thousand year history, Windsor has only seen action once, during the reign of King John. The balance of power between a monarch and his nobles was an ongoing source of conflict until the end of the Wars of the Roses. A strong king kept his barons in check, a weak king was subject to his barons flexing their muscles and demanding greater autonomy from the Crown. In 1215 many of England's barons rebelled against the erratic King John, and forced him to sign the Magna Carta, a document that conceded much power to the barons and enshrined that concession as law. Magna Carta was signed on Runnymede, an island in the Thames 3 miles downstream from Windsor. John immediately attempted to revoke Magna Carta, starting a civil war with his barons. A French army was sent to the aid of the barons, and Windsor was besieged. The castle was never under serious threat, and held out until the conflict ended with John's death the following year.

5 Follow the footpath into a lane, and keep ahead, past Eton College Boathouse, to reach a road in front of the Waterman Arms. Keep ahead, the Waterman to your left, to reach the main road beside the George Inn. Turn right back onto the bridge and the start of the walk.

To visit the castle, cross the bridge and follow the road around to the left to the castle entrance.

Windsor Castle is open daily apart from Easter and Christmas, from 9.45 am until 5.15 pm (4.15 pm November to February). The State Apartments can be visited most times of the year, and the magnificent St George's Chapel is open daily. There is an admission charge.

Oxford: The Founding of the University (1167)

Length: 3 or 4 miles

The Radcliffe Camera

> **HOW TO GET THERE:** The walk starts from Oxford railway station but the route could be picked up at any suitable town centre point, e.g. the Martyrs' Memorial.
>
> **PARKING:** Parking is not easy in Oxford itself, but there are a number of park-and-ride points on the ring road.
>
> **MAP:** OS Landranger 164 (GR 505063).

INTRODUCTION

A fascinating walk through central Oxford, the route passes all the city's most historically important landmarks, including the colleges, the Ashmolean Museum, the Bodleian Library, the Radcliffe Camera and the Botanical Gardens. The loop around Christ Church meadow can be avoided by a short-cut, but is a lovely walk along the rivers Cherwell and Thames that makes a contrast to the city streets.

HISTORICAL BACKGROUND

Oxford stands on a gravel terrace above a place where the rivers Thames and Cherwell meet and can be crossed. This is prime agricultural land, and there has been a settlement here from Neolithic times onwards. In Saxon times it became an important administrative centre and a stronghold against Danish invasions. Its central location between the kingdoms of Mercia, Wessex and the Danelaw made it a natural council site for solving territorial disputes. Oxford was a market centre for a rural hinterland, containing the town houses of rural estate owners, and also developing industry based upon weaving and metalwork. By 1066 Oxford was the sixth largest town in England.

There was little resistance to the Norman Conquest in Oxfordshire. Ecclesiastical estates survived the Conquest largely unscathed, but the Saxon nobility were dispossessed and replaced by minor Norman landlords. Political and commercial life centred on nearby Woodstock, and so Oxford declined dramatically as the Saxon town was exploited by Norman interlopers. Not until the 1130s did the town start to recover.

The Norman kings looked to the Continent for learning and culture, but in 1167 all English students were expelled from Paris University, part of deteriorating relations with France. Students drifted to Oxford, where the Priory of St Frideswide and Osney Abbey were already teaching centres. Teachers followed students, new colleges were endowed, and the nucleus of England's first university came into being. The steady influx of often rowdy students was resented by the townsfolk, culminating in a two-day pitched battle in 1355 which left 62 students dead. Royal intervention resulted, which put effective control of the town and its trade into the hands of the university.

Oxford was the centre of bitter religious dispute in Tudor times, and both

Catholics and Protestants died in the town for their faith. Although the monastic colleges were suppressed during the Dissolution, the institutions survived and many were refounded under new names. In 1546 Oxford became a city, and more colleges were built.

In 1642, after he had fled from London, King Charles I chose Oxford, with its position in the centre of England, as his capital. Although the city was Parliamentarian, the university was staunchly Royalist, and Oxford remained Charles' capital until he fled in 1646, leaving a city ridden with debt and disease. Gradually the city rebuilt itself, now without the rivalry between town and university, and Oxford returned to normality.

THE WALK

1 With your back to the railway station, cross the bus station and turn right to the traffic lights. Turn left and walk along the left-hand side of the wide road towards the Royal Oxford Hotel. Cross Rewley Road at the traffic lights and keep ahead along Hythe Bridge Road. Follow the road over a bridge crossing the

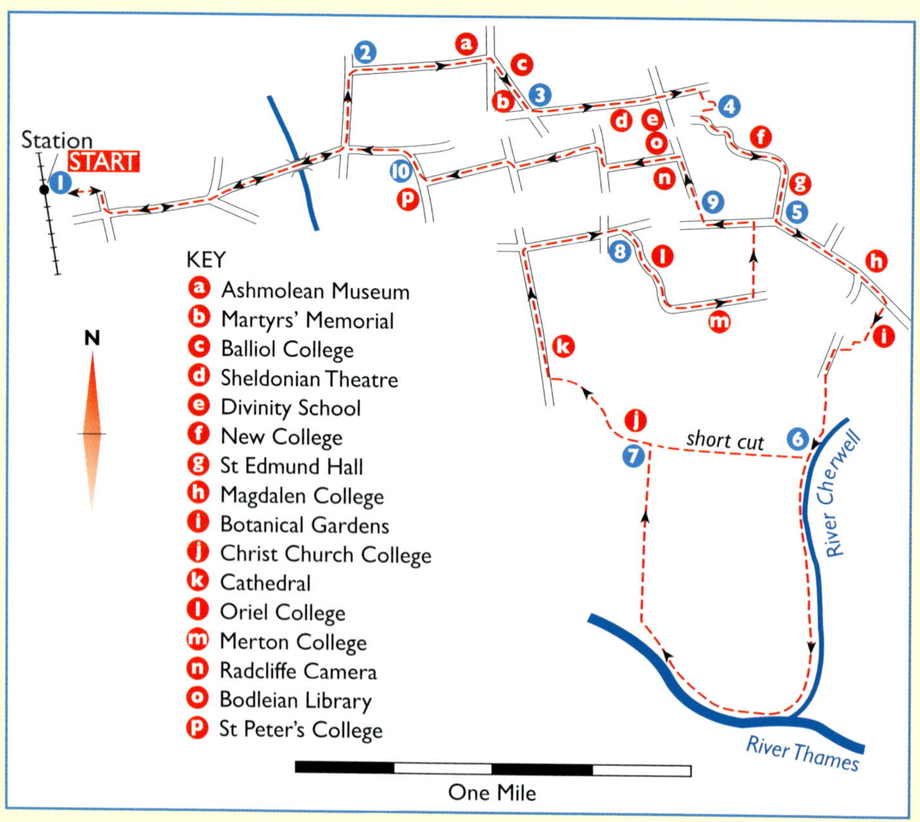

Oxford Canal to traffic lights. Here turn left and go along Worcester Street.

2   Turn right at traffic lights and walk along Beaumont Street, soon passing the Ashmolean Museum **(a)** on your left.

The Ashmolean is the oldest museum in Britain. It was founded in 1683 when Elias Ashmole donated various collections. The current building dates from 1840, and houses mainly natural history, antiquities, archaeology, and artefacts from abroad. Open Tuesday to Saturday 10 am to 4 pm, Sunday 2 pm to 4 pm. Admission free.

At the end of Beaumont Street, cross the main road to the Martyrs' Memorial **(b)**.

The Martyrs' Memorial stands upon the spot where Bishops Latimer and Ridley, and Archbishop Cranmer, were burned as heretics in 1555 for refusing to renounce the Protestant religion. Over 300 people were burned to death upon the orders of Queen Mary as she attempted to reverse the religious revolution of her father and brother, and return England to the Catholic Church. Latimer died with the prophetic words, 'We shall this day light such a candle, by God's grace in England, as I trust shall never be put out.' Certainly the burnings were counter-productive, leading to a wave of revulsion against the excesses of Mary's counter-reformation.

Cross over, past the memorial to the gates of Balliol College **(c)** opposite.

The stones still show scorch marks from the fires that burned the Protestant martyrs. Balliol is one of Oxford's three oldest colleges. It was founded in 1263 by the Scottish noble John Balliol, as an act of penance after being excommunicated by the Bishop of Durham, whom he had kidnapped. Balliol was originally a theological college and was for centuries reserved for poor students. Open daily 10 am to 6 pm.

Turn right and walk along the walls of Balliol College. At the end of the street, opposite Boswells' Department Store, turn left along Broad Street.

3   Continue along Broad Street, to pass the round Sheldonian Theatre **(d)** on your right.

The domed, circular building of the Sheldonian Theatre was the first architectural work by the young Christopher Wren in the 1660s, at that time Professor of Astronomy at London. Architecture was in its infancy as a discipline, and Wren studied abroad before returning to become the first professional architect in Britain. He modelled the Sheldonian upon classical Roman open-air theatres, and incorporated classical columns into its design.

Continue to the traffic lights. The porticoed building on your right houses the Divinity School **(e)**.

The Divinity School was built between 1427 and 1483. It was the first purpose-built lecture room in the university, teaching having been done previously in hired rooms, created for the study of the most important subject of that time. It had no single benefactor but was built largely by public subscription. It was used between 1642 and 1646 as the meeting place for Charles I's House of Commons, an essentially powerless body established as a rival to Parliament to demonstrate the king's democratic credentials. The Divinity School is open Monday to Friday 9 am to 4.45 pm, and Saturday 9 am to 12 noon, and can be seen as part of a visit to the Bodleian Library, of which buildings it is now part.

Cross the road at the traffic lights and keep ahead along Holywell Street. In 100 yards, turn right down a cobbled alley (Bath Place). At the end of the alley, at the gates to the Bath Place Hotel, turn left through an arch, signed 'Turf Tavern'. Follow the alleyway as it winds between buildings to a road.

4 Turn left and follow the road as it bends right and then left. At the gates to New College Chapel, turn right under an arch. Pass through a barrier and then turn left again with the road. Follow the lane, passing New College **(f)** on your left.

New College was founded in 1379 by William of Wykeham, who wanted to ensure that there were enough educated men to serve as parish priests in the wake of the Black Death. It was to have been called St Mary's College of Winchester, but as a St Mary's college existed already (later Oriel) it was nicknamed 'New College'. Wykeham instructed that students for his new college should come from his other foundation, Winchester grammar school. It was built as a single entity, rather than evolving piecemeal, and was the first college to have been built around a quadrangle, later to become the accepted design. In the grounds of New College there are mounds of earth, raised as gun embrasures for the Royalist Cannon in the defence of the city against Parliamentary assault. The college is open 2 pm to 5 pm during term, 11 am to 5 pm during vacations.

Turn right with the lane, passing St Edmund Hall **(g)** on your left.

St Edmund Hall is Oxford's sole surviving medieval hall of residence, only granted college status in 1957. It had no single founder but was set up in 1238 by a group of students as a boarding-house for undergraduates. It is named after St Edmund of Abingdon, the first Oxford graduate to become Archbishop of Canterbury. Open during daylight hours.

5 Follow the lane out to the High Street, and turn left. Continue along the High Street over traffic lights, passing Magdalen College **(h)** on your left.

Magdalen College was founded in 1458. Its bell tower, Oxford's most dominant landmark, was added in 1492 and attributed to Cardinal Wolsey, bursar there at the time. During the Civil War the tower was used as a watchtower, and Royalist defenders used it to stone Parliamentarian troops trying to cross the bridge over the Cherwell. In the period 1685-88 Magdalen was the centre of opposition to James II's Catholic policies. Open daily 2 pm to 6 pm.

In 30 yards, after the entrance to Magdelen College Chapel, look for a bricked-up archway in the wall of the college on your left.

This blocked-up doorway was where, in the Middle Ages, beggars used to queue for scraps from the college kitchen.

Cross over the road at the beggars' gate. Turn left for a few yards, then turn right through a gateway leading into the Botanical Gardens **(i)**.

The Botanical Gardens are England's oldest teaching gardens. They were founded in 1621 by the Earl of Derby on the site of an old Jewish cemetery, to grow plants used for medicinal purposes. In the 17th century both Pepys and Evelyn describe the gardens in their diaries, and they have changed little since then. The gateway, by Inigo Jones, has statues of both Charles I and Charles II. Open March to October, 2 pm to 5 pm; November to February 9 am to 4.30 pm. There is an admission charge.

Turn right, walking with the outside wall of the Botanical Gardens on your left hand, and follow the wall into Rose Lane. Turn left along the lane and go through gates into Christ Church Meadows. Bear left along a broad drive, soon reaching the river Cherwell on your left. Where the drive turns right, keep straight ahead, following the river.

6 For the short cut, turn right with the drive and rejoin the route at point 7 below. Otherwise, follow the path alongside the river, eventually joining the Thames. Keep ahead along the broad Thames, but 100 yards short of a stone-arched road bridge, turn right along a broad drive away from the river. Follow the drive to a T-junction.

7 Turn left at the T-junction (keep straight on if rejoining from the short cut). On your right is Christ Church College **(j)**.

Christ Church, Oxford's most majestic college, was founded in 1525 as 'Cardinal College' by Cardinal Wolsey, whose statue stands above the main door, and refounded (and renamed) in 1532 by Henry VIII. The Tom Tower was created by Sir Christopher Wren and the bell it houses, Great Tom, tolls at 9.05 pm (the time students originally had to be in), a total of 101 times , once for each of the original students at the college. During the Civil War, Christ Church was used by Charles I as his court and home. Since 1546 its chapel has served as Oxford's cathedral. Open daily 1.30 pm to 4.30 pm.

At the end of the drive in 50 yards, go ahead through the car park and bear right along a lane, the walls of Christ Church on your right. Follow the cobbled lane through an arch to a road. Turn right along the road, passing the gates leading to the cathedral **(k)**.

This is England's smallest cathedral and parts date from the 12th century. It contains monuments to Royalists who died in the Civil War, and stained-glass windows which survived the Commonwealth, including the Becket window dating from 1320.

Continue along the road, passing the museum on your right, to reach traffic lights at a crossroads. Turn right along High Street. After 200 yards turn right into King Edward Street.

8 Follow King Edward Street to its end, passing Oriel College **(l)** on your left.

Oriel College was founded in 1326 by Edward II, in thanks for his escape from the battle of Bannockburn. The building was greatly restored in the 17th century and the original architecture lost. One of Oriel's scholars, the colonial pioneer Cecil Rhodes, left a vast sum of money in his will to provide scholarships bearing his name. Open daily 2 pm to 5 pm.

Turn left into Merton Street, and keep ahead along the road, soon cobbled, and pass Merton College **(m)** on your right.

Merton is one of Oxford's oldest colleges, founded in 1264 by Walter de Merton, Chancellor to Henry III, to provide education for 20 students, including eight of his nephews. Although Balliol predates it, Merton was the first purpose-built college, where students could lodge and were supervised by qualified authorities, and was to become the model for colleges in the future. The Gatehouse Tower has statues of Chancellor Merton and Henry III, and provided lodgings for Queen Henrietta Maria during the Civil War. Open Monday to Friday, 2 pm to 5 pm; weekends 10 am to 5 pm.

Opposite the end of Merton College, and just past an ivy-covered building on your left, turn left along a cobbled bridleway through University College. Follow the bridleway out to the High Street. Cross the road and turn left. Just before pedestrian lights, turn right through bollards into Catte Street.

9 Keep ahead along Catte Street, passing the Radcliffe Camera **(n)** on your left.

The Radcliffe Camera was built in 1748 by James Gibbs, using a concept thought up by Nicholas Hawksmoor, as the first round library in England. It was named after Dr Radcliffe, who left £40,000 in his will for building a new library.

Turn left between the Camera on your left and the Bodleian Library **(o)** on your right.

The Bodleian Library is one of the oldest libraries in Europe, and in England is second only in size to the British Museum. The first library in Oxford was a collection of divinity texts donated by Thomas Cobham, Bishop of Worcester. This collection was dramatically enlarged in 1447 when Humphrey, Duke of Gloucester, the disgraced Protector to Henry VI, donated his extensive library to Oxford University, laying the foundation of today's Bodleian Library. This collection is still in existence, housed today above the Divinity School. In 1602 Thomas Bodley, a graduate of Magdalen College, endowed the library with over 2,000 extra books, and gave the building its name. Entry to the Library is by reading ticket only, but the Divinity School and Exhibition Rooms are open Monday to Friday 9 am to 4.45 pm, and Saturday 9am to 12 noon.

Keep ahead along Brasenose Lane. At the end turn right into Turl Street. Turn left into Ship Street and follow it to a crossroads. Keep ahead into St Michael's Street and follow it to a T-junction. Turn left for a few yards along New Inn Hall Street to reach the modern buildings of St Peter's College **(p)** on your right.

St Peter's is one of Oxford's newer colleges, dating from 1961. It stands on the site of New Inn Hall, a rooming house for the 16th-century university, that during the Civil War was used as a royal mint by the desperately cash-starved Royalists.

10 Retrace your steps along New Inn Hall Street, passing the entrance to St Michael's Street on your right, and come to a T-junction. Turn left along George Street and keep straight on over the traffic lights. Retrace your outward steps over the canal bridge, to reach the railway station on your right after 300 yards.

GREAT COXWELL AND THE WEALTH OF THE MEDIEVAL CHURCH

Length: 6 miles

The impressive medieval barn at Great Coxwell

HOW TO GET THERE: The walk starts on the village green at Coleshill, which is on the B4019, midway between Highworth and Faringdon.

PARKING: There is ample street parking on and around the green.

MAP: OS Landranger 163 (GR 237937).

INTRODUCTION

The Great Barn at Great Coxwell, called 'the finest piece of architecture in England' by William Morris in the 19th century, is the focus for this walk through pleasant countryside with wide views, on the way passing the Iron Age hillfort of Badbury Rings. The return is through fields and parkland to the village green at Coleshill.

HISTORICAL BACKGROUND

Medieval monasteries were not only religious centres, but also played a significant part in the secular economy of England during the Middle Ages. The secular community had an obligation to support religious houses with tithes, in the form of money and agricultural produce. But those houses were also major feudal landlords in their own right, possessing 10% of the land and 20% of England's annual income. In Norman England one person in every hundred was directly employed by a religious house. The opulence of the medieval Church is spectacularly demonstrated at Great Coxwell, with its tithe barn built by the monks of the Cistercian Abbey of Beaulieu.

The original home of the Cistercians was Citeaux Abbey in France, but the 'White Monks', named after the robes they wore, spread throughout the territory of the Norman kings. The first Cistercian house in England was founded in 1128 at Waverley in Surrey, and others soon followed. The Cistercians believed that their monasteries should be far from other habitations, and that their monks should remain free from everyday distractions. They were also shrewd business managers however, and their religious houses soon had an infrastructure of farms and granges, run by lay brothers, which produced wealth for the parent monastery.

In 1203 King John gave the royal manor of Faringdon to the Cistercians, to support a new abbey. The abbey itself soon moved to Beaulieu in the New Forest, but the manor, which covered a huge tract in Oxfordshire, Berkshire and Wiltshire, was retained to generate wealth and income. The Cistercians often

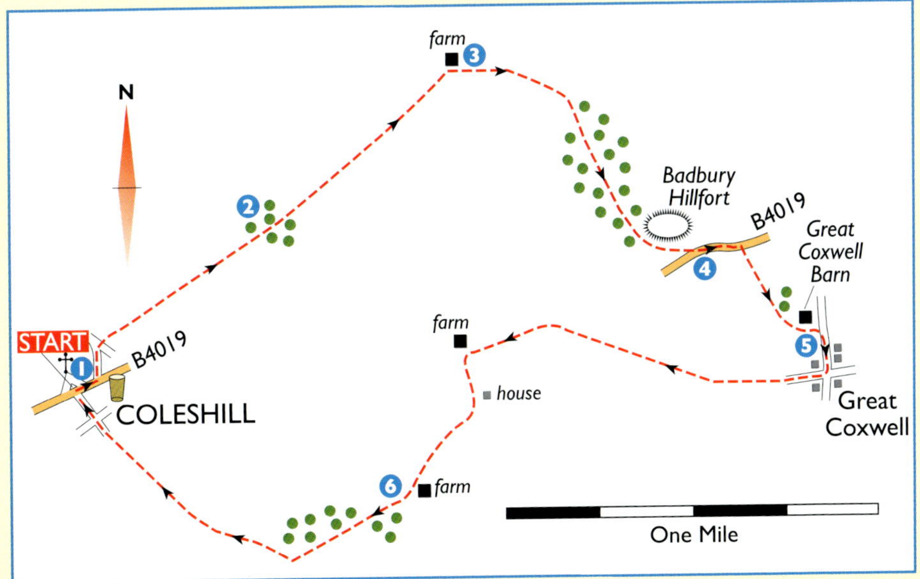

pioneered new developments in both the production and sale of goods, and were major innovators in the development of commercial wool production in England.

THE WALK

1 Standing on the village green, with your back to the church, turn left along the main road, past the Radnor Arms. Immediately turn left along a minor road. At a T-junction in 150 yards, cross over the road to a gravel drive more or less opposite. DO NOT turn right with the drive but go forward through a double field gate. Keep ahead up the side of the field, a hedge on your left. At the far end go through a gap into the next field and continue ahead, still with the hedge on your left. In the bottom left-hand corner of the field keep straight on through a gap into woods.

2 Follow the path through the edge of woods for 120 yards. Where the path curves right, keep straight on across a footbridge to a stile into a field. Keep ahead up the side of the field, a hedge on your left. At the end, keep ahead across a stile and along an enclosed footpath. Cross a stile and a footbridge and turn left along the edge of the field, turning a corner and following the left-hand field boundary to a stile on the left, just beyond the first telegraph pole. Go half right across the next field, aiming at a house chimney seen on the far side. Cross one stile and then a second one 20 yards later, on to a track.

Turn right along the track for a few yards. Keep straight on across a drive and down a track for a few more yards, to cross a second drive to reach double gates leading into a field. All the time you are keeping to the right of farm buildings.

3 Keep straight on along the edge of the next field, fence on your left, to cross a bridge. Turn left for 10 yards, then turn right, following the field boundary towards woods. Enter the woods and follow a clear path uphill. Go over a cross-track and keep uphill, now with a wire fence on your left. Soon go over another cross-track and keep ahead uphill, joining a broader track and continuing, still with a fence on your left. When the fence ends, keep ahead up a broad track. The track soon narrows, but keep ahead, avoiding side turns. Keep to the right of a fenced enclosure and follow the path as it swings left and uphill. Soon the ramparts of Badbury hillfort are reached on your left.

Badbury hillfort is an Iron Age enclosure, built by the Dobunni tribe, who occupied the valleys of the upper Thames and lower Severn. Like all hillforts, it was not permanently occupied, but built to provide shelter in times of emergency for the farmers who lived in the valleys around. The fort would also have acted as a centre for trade and as a local administrative centre for the tribe. Badbury was subsidiary to nearby Uffington fort (see Walk 1), just 5 miles to the south. The presence of two large forts so close together is an indication of how thickly populated the area was in the Iron Age, and also demonstrates the affluence of the Dobunni.

Follow the track to a gate into a car park. Keep ahead along the car park and down the entrance drive to a road.

4 Just before reaching the road turn left at a waymark post into a field. Immediately turn right and follow the hedge, road beyond, for 200 yards. Leave the field at the second gateway. Cross the road to a footpath sign for 'Great Coxwell' and cross the stile. Follow a broad path across a field, soon joining trees on your left hand, and walk down the slope. Some 50 yards short of a gate at the bottom of the field, turn left over a stile into the trees. Follow the footpath across the corner of the wood, to a footbridge and stile into a field. Turn left along the edge of the field to a stile on the left, leading to Great Coxwell Barn.

The Great Barn at Great Coxwell is 144 ft long by 38 ft wide, and has a floor area of 5,502 square ft. The walls of Cotswold stone are 4 ft thick. The aisled roof is 48 ft high, of a design similar to a hammer beam roof, of a size and complexity unequalled in a medieval English secular building. The majesty of the building inspired William Morris, founder of the 19th-century Arts and Crafts Movement, to call it the 'finest piece of architecture in England'. Most of the stonework and timbers are still the medieval originals.

The barn was built around 1300 to 1310, to house the produce of the grange, or monastic farm, of Great Coxwell. This grange was one of a number owned by Beaulieu Abbey. The produce included a quarter of all of the abbey's grain, mainly wheat and oats but also rye, grown on the grange's own lands, some 120 tons annually. Wool, produced both from the abbey's own flocks of 6,000 sheep on the nearby Cotswolds and Berkshire Downs, and bought in from other farmers, was collected here for resale to wool merchants. Livestock were also housed here, and on average four tons of cheese and six tons of butter were produced on the grange. The four tons of honey produced each year in the grange's hives were stored here. Much of this produce was paid as feudal rent to the grange by the neighbourhood, although some was produced by hired labour and some bought in from other farmers. Virtually all of the goods stored here were sold in local and national markets, the cash proceeds being sent to the parent abbey. When it is remembered that this was just one grange owned by just one monastery, then the sheer wealth of the medieval Church begins to become apparent.

Open at any reasonable time, there is a small entrance fee (free to National Trust members).

5 After viewing the barn, pass between the barn and outbuildings to a road and turn right into the village of Great Coxwell. Ignore a turn to the left, but on reaching a staggered crossroads, turn right down Puddleduck Lane, which leads to a gate. Go through, passing barns on your left, and keep straight on along a track. After ½ mile follow the track through a gate into a field and to a gate on the far side. Go through and keep ahead along the track, which is soon enclosed. At the end, go through a gate to a T-junction of tracks.

REFRESHMENTS

The Radnor Arms in Coleshill offers a good range of beers and food, and has a beer garden and a car park. Telephone: 01793 762366.

Turn left, away from a farm, and follow a track curving left. In 150 yards pass a house on your left. Just before a gate ahead, turn right through a gate into a field. Follow the right-hand edge of the field, trees on your right, to a stile in the top right-hand corner. Cross the stile and keep ahead along the top of a field, a hedge on your right. Just before a farm, cross a stile on the right. Resume your line of advance to pass the farm on your left hand.

6   At the end of the farm building, keep ahead along a concrete drive for 10 yards to a T-junction with a farm road. Cross the road to a gate opposite and keep ahead along a broad track across a field, soon with trees on your left. When the trees end, keep straight on along the track, soon with trees on your right. Follow the track along the top of the next two fields. At the start of the third field, where the trees on the right end, DO NOT follow the obvious track across the field. Instead turn right around the corner of the trees.

Keep ahead for a few yards, then go quarter-left across the edge of the field, aiming for a clump of trees on the skyline ahead. Pass close to the left of the trees and then maintain your line of advance down the field, to cross a stile visible directly ahead. Keep ahead to a stile on the opposite side of the narrow field. Cross this double stile and footbridge, then keep straight on across the field towards the buildings of Coleshill seen ahead. On the far side of a huge pasture, cross a stile and keep ahead across the next field to go through a gate, just to the right of a house. Go along a short track to a T-junction of lanes. Cross over and keep ahead along the lane for 200 yards, to reach the main road at the village green.

Hurley Priory and the Dissolution of the Monasteries (1538)

Length: 3 miles

Hurley church is of Saxon origin

HOW TO GET THERE: The walk starts by the church in Hurley, which is just north of the A4130, 3 miles west of Maidenhead and 6 miles south of Junction 4 of the M40.

PARKING: There is a free car park next to the church.

MAP: OS Landranger 175 (GR 825841).

INTRODUCTION

From the village of Hurley this walk passes through fields and along quiet lanes before reaching the towpath alongside the river Thames. After visiting a Victorian lock that made the Thames navigable, you find the ruins of Hurley Priory, including an 11th-century dovecote, and return to explore the church, with its splendid monuments. Route-finding is easy, terrain is flat and good underfoot.

HISTORICAL BACKGROUND

In the reign of Henry VIII an increasing desire to reform the organisation of the Church coincided with the king's political needs. For religious houses such as Hurley Priory, the results were disastrous.

During the Middle Ages the Church was the richest landowner in England after the king. Many religious houses performed important work helping the poor and needy, but all too often the Church neglected its pastoral duties and used its spiritual power to protect its secular interests. Henry VIII was a devout Catholic, who had been awarded the title of 'Defender of the Faith' by the Pope for his erudite and vigorous defence of Catholicism against the doctrines of Luther, and had no inclination to join the attack on the Church, known as the Reformation,

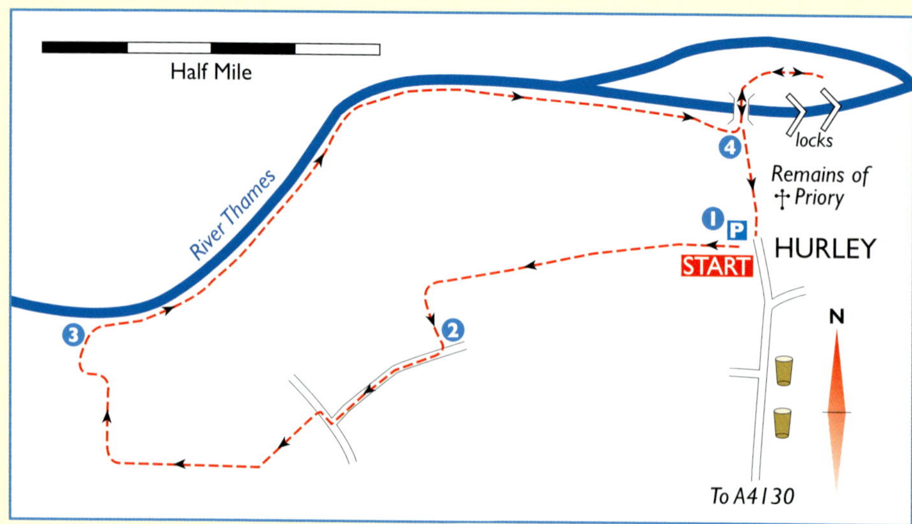

that was sweeping Northern Europe. However, dynastic considerations were to force his hand.

For most of the previous century, England had been racked by the civil war later known as the Wars of the Roses, as powerful factions vied to control the Crown. The reign of Henry's father, Henry VII, had seen several pretenders to the throne raising rebellion, and Henry VIII's own right to the throne had been contested. Henry was desperate for an heir whose claim to the throne would be undisputed, and this meant a son. Although there was no constitutional reason why a queen should not rule England, it had never happened successfully, and it was doubted that a woman would be strong enough to rule. Many years of happy marriage had only given Henry one live child, a daughter Mary, and with no prospect of a son, the spectre of his dynasty being challenged after his death drove Henry to desperate measures. In 1527 he decided to divorce his beloved wife, Queen Catherine of Aragon, and marry the younger Anne Boleyn, who held out the prospect of producing a male child.

Unfortunately for the king, the Pope rejected Henry's ingenious arguments as to why his marriage to Catherine was illegal and refused to grant a divorce. To influence the Pope, Henry started to put pressure on the Church in England, increasingly curbing its powers and attacking its privileges. For five years the Pope resisted Henry's steadily increasing campaign against the Church, until in 1533 he finally excommunicated Henry. The king responded by declaring himself Supreme Head of the Church in England and the break with Rome was complete. Over the next five years the land and wealth of the Church was subject to widespread confiscation, and in the process known as the Dissolution of the Monasteries most religious houses were closed, their buildings demolished and the monks and nuns turned out to fend for themselves.

THE WALK

① From the car park entrance, with your back to the road, go down the left side of the car park and then keep ahead along an enclosed footpath for 30 yards. Go through a gate and keep ahead along a tarmac drive, passing the entrance to a caravan park on your right. In 600 yards, at the end of a field on your left, turn left over a stile at a fingerpost. Walk along the field edge, the hedge close on your right, towards a mock half-timbered house on the far side of the field. Cross a stile and keep ahead along an enclosed footpath, the house on your left, to reach a lane.

② Turn right along the lane for 500 yards to a T-junction of tracks. Go half right across the road, then through a kissing gate. Walk down the side of the field. Cross a footbridge. Keep close to the right-hand edge of the field and walk around to a second footbridge at a waymark post. Cross two bridges in rapid succession and go along the side of the field, hedge on your right, to a fingerpost. Turn right through a kissing gate and walk along the side of the field, a fence on your left. At the end of the field go through a kissing gate and turn left, to follow an enclosed footpath. Follow the path along the edge of a garden and out to a riverside drive, where turn right.

3 Go through a gate and keep ahead along the riverside footpath. Cross a grassy parking area opposite a caravan site and keep ahead along the river bank. Where the open meadow ends, and after passing a weir, keep ahead, fences and houses on your right. Climb with the path to a bridge on your left. Cross the bridge and turn right along the footpath to the lock, where there is a picnic area and toilets.

At Hurley, the Thames in its natural state dropped a considerable height in a short space, and as a result it was fast flowing, with difficult currents. This made it impassable for boats, one of many such obstacles which rendered the Thames un-navigable. The first lock was put in here in the middle of the 18th century, and at the same time the weir just upstream was constructed, making it possible for boats to pass upstream and thus connecting the upper Thames valley with London. The present lock was built in 1856, and has since been modernised.

Look to the right across the lock and you will see the back of a long old building, in front of the church. This was part of the refectory of Hurley Priory, which we see more closely later in the walk.

4 Retrace your steps to re-cross the bridge. At the far end of the bridge, go down steps. Follow the footpath ahead, in 5 yards crossing a small footbridge.

The marshy area on the right is the remains of fishponds, built by the monks. Fish were an important part of the diet in the Middle Ages, when meat was an expensive commodity which was also seasonal, since it could not be easily preserved through the summer months. Fish, if properly farmed, were available all year round, and were doubly valuable to religious communities in that they could be eaten on Fridays and during Lent.

Continue along the footpath.

Note the old wall on your left. This is the wall that surrounded Hurley Priory, parts of which are still the medieval original.

Follow the footpath out to a lane.

On your right is a modern house, 'Tithecote'. Look through the ornamental lychgate at the house itself. This was once the tithe barn of the priory. Like all religious establishments, Hurley Priory was entitled to one tenth of the produce of the locality, and although some of this tithe was taken as money, much was taken as produce – meat, grain and vegetables – which was used partly to feed the monks and partly for resale. This produce was stored in tithe barns. The tithe barn here was converted into a house in the 20th century.

To the left of the barn stands a dovecote, built in 1087 and now a Grade I listed building. Doves were bred by the monks of Hurley for their meat. Under the laws that protected religious establishments, the local peasantry were not allowed to kill the doves under pain of severe punishment: the doves however, were allowed to eat whatever they wanted, including the peasants' grain.

Turn left towards the church.

Look through the arch to the left of the church. This arch, rebuilt in 1970, today leads to a private house, but the original led into the Priory quadrangle, the outline of which can still be clearly seen today. On the north side of the quadrangle (your left) is the old refectory, the dining hall of the monks. The lower half of the building dates from 1087, whilst the upper half was rebuilt in the early 1500s. Today the refectory is a private house. Facing you across the quadrangle is a modern house called 'The Cloisters'. This stands on the site of the original chapter house and dormitory of the Priory.

Along the wall of the church (your right), can be seen the remains of sawn-off beams set into the church wall, about 9 ft above the ground. This marks the line of a covered walkway, an 'ambulatory', along this side of the cloister.

Go through the gate to the right of the church and keep ahead to the church entrance.

The first church at Hurley was built around AD 700, by order of St Birinus. A small village grew up around the church, eventually part of the estates of Lord Esgar, Master of Horse to Edward the Confessor. After the Norman Conquest, William gave the estate to one of his loyal supporters, Geoffrey de Mandeville. Geoffrey's wife, Leceline, was a devout Christian, and encouraged her husband to renovate and expand the Saxon church.

In 1086, at Leceline's request, the church was dedicated by Bishop Osmund of Old Sarum (modern Salisbury), as a priory, and given to the Benedictine Order. The monks of Hurley set about increasing the size of the church, building monastic buildings around it inside a walled enclosure, with barns, dovecotes and a mill outside the priory walls. We have seen the often well-preserved remains of those buildings earlier.

Hurley Priory grew in importance, and in the 14th century the church was extended eastwards to almost double its length, with side aisles being added to the eastern extension. The monastery was dissolved after 1536 and the lands bought by John Lovelace. Much of the eastern extension of the church was demolished for materials to build the first Ladye Place Mansion (its successor faces the church today).

It is worthwhile visiting the church, which retains the long narrow shape of its Saxon origins. The north wall is still the original Saxon, whilst most of the remainder is early Norman. Look above the outside of the south-west door, through which you enter: the beautiful zigzag moulding, although restored, is original Norman. There is also a splendid monument to the Lovelace family inside the church. John Lovelace bought the manor of Hurley in 1545. The monument is to his son and grandson, both named Richard, the latter being knighted by Elizabeth I for his services in Ireland, and becoming 1st Baron Lovelace in 1627. His grandson, John, the 3rd Baron, plotted the overthrow of James II in the Glorious Revolution (see Walk 13).

After visiting the church, with your back to the church door, keep ahead on a path through the churchyard.

There are several ancient yew trees in the graveyard, suggesting that this may have been a site of worship even before the Saxon building. The yew had great religious significance in pre-Christian Britain, when deities were to be found in forests and groves, marshes, lakes, rivers and springs, and the druids, religious leaders of great importance, conducted services in groves. The yew tree has dark red berries fruiting at the time of Midwinter's Day, when the world is at its coldest and darkest, and thus had a special significance for ceremonies based around renewing the Earth and calling the sun back. Yew trees and their berries became incorporated into the later Christian symbols of Christmas. In an attempt to suppress pagan religions, the Christians often built chapels on sites of pagan worship, and ancient yews are often to be found in churchyards.

Exit by a gate in the wall on your right, to come out to a small grassy triangle.

In 1976 the Lordship of the Manor of Hurley and the common land associated with it (which includes this triangle) was bought by the people of Hurley, to be preserved from development.

To visit either of the pubs, keep ahead along the lane for 200 yards. To return to the car park, turn right.

STONOR PARK AND THE ELIZABETHAN COLD WAR

Length: 4½ miles

Stonor House

HOW TO GET THERE: The walk starts from the gates of Stonor Park, which is on a minor road 3 miles north of the A4130, reached by travelling north-west out of Henley-on-Thames for 2 miles towards Nettlebed, and turning right.

PARKING: There is limited roadside parking in lay-bys, between Stonor Park gates and the village of Stonor just to the south.

MAP: OS Landranger 175 (GR 738892).

INTRODUCTION

This walk crosses beautiful rolling farmland interspersed with woodland paths, before entering the grounds of Stonor Park and returning past centuries-old Stonor House. Look out for the herd of fallow deer that inhabits the park. There are two steep ascents on the route.

HISTORICAL BACKGROUND

The Reformation divided Europe into two camps ideologically, and religion became a cause or at least a veneer upon many of the conflicts between and within nations. The introduction of the Reformation into England had been primarily for political and dynastic reasons, and both Henry VIII and later his daughter Elizabeth were content to accept a public display of loyalty from their subjects whilst turning a blind eye to continued Catholic worship in private.

By the 1570s England had become the foremost of the Protestant countries of northern Europe, and the Catholic powers, led by Spain, were determined to destabilise the throne prior to replacing Elizabeth with a suitably Catholic monarch. English Catholics were seen as tools in this cold war. In 1570 Elizabeth was excommunicated by the Pope and her subjects released from loyalty to her. English Catholic priests were trained in Flanders by the exiled cleric William Allen, and from 1574 onwards smuggled back into England to spearhead the old religion. These were joined in 1580 by Jesuit priests, determined to ferment discontent. Catholic writings were printed and spread throughout England to

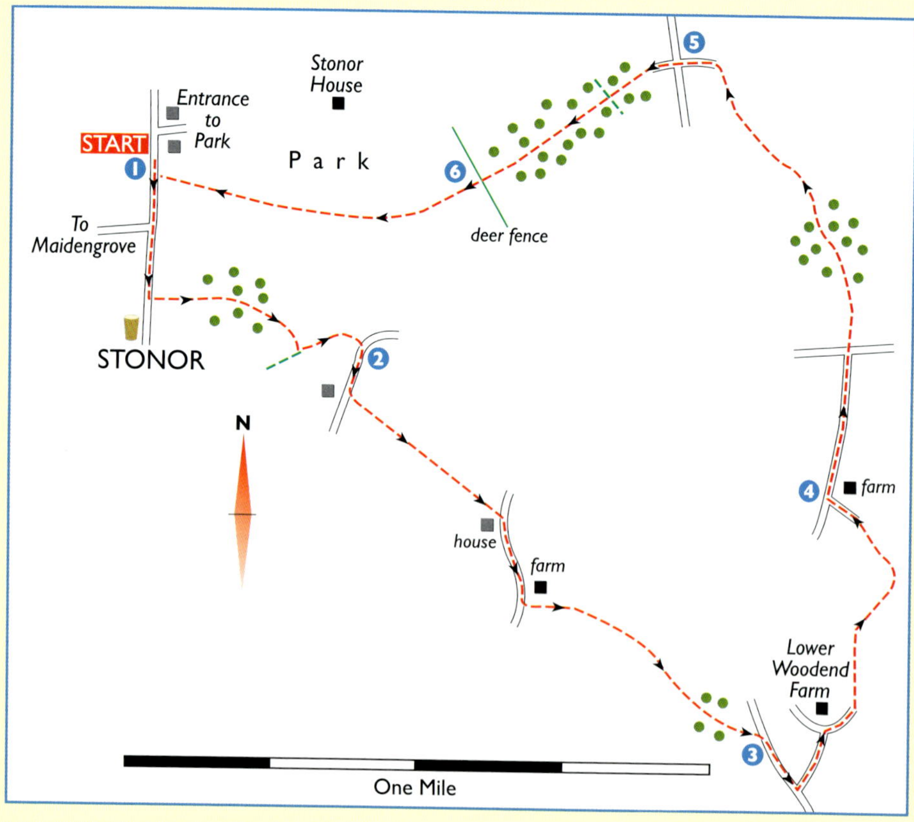

devoted Catholics. By 1584 Spain, with the support of the Pope, was ready to turn the cold war into a hot one, and started building an armada with which to invade England. It was assumed that English Catholics would rise up in support of their co-religionists.

Members of the Stonor family were devout Catholics and continued to make a defiant public proclamation of their faith throughout the reign of Elizabeth, openly celebrating the mass in their household chapel. As such, they were amongst the handful of people to publicly deny the Church of England. They also openly abetted the Catholic cause in its cold war against England. Stonor Park became a refuge, not only for English Catholics fleeing persecution, but also for Jesuit priests sent from the Continent to foment rebellion. The Jesuit priest Edmund Campion, trained by William Allen, used Stonor Park in 1581 as his base from which to spread the Catholic faith round the county.

For their actions, the family were heavily taxed, and their lands confiscated. All public office was denied them, and they were forbidden to educate their children in England unless at Protestant schools. The Stonors suffered for their religious beliefs from 1533 until the Catholic Emancipation Act was passed in 1829, when prohibitions against the Catholic faith were finally removed. In 1838 Thomas Stonor was allowed to become Baron Camoys, a title inherited from his great-grandmother but which had been denied the family until then.

THE WALK

1 From the gates of Stonor Park, walk along the road towards Stonor village, with the fence of the park on your left. Pass a turning to Maidengrove on the right. Immediately past the house named 'Gable End' on the left, turn left into a bridleway. Follow the enclosed path as it climbs steeply uphill through woods, with a deer fence on your left. At the top of the slope, at a T-junction, turn left onto a track, still following the deer fence on your left. Follow the track out to a lane and turn right.

2 Go along the lane for 100 yards and then, opposite the gate to a cottage, turn left over a stile. Go half right across the field to cross a stile on the far side. Keep straight on, aiming initially to the right of power lines seen in mid-field. Go through a kissing gate and keep ahead, aiming to the left of a house. Go through a kissing gate beside a field gate and turn right along the metalled drive beyond, passing through three sets of gates.

Pass a duck pond on your right and a farm on the left. Shortly after, at white gates at the end of the farm, turn left through a gate and follow the track into a farmyard. Go half right across the farmyard, aiming for the continuation of the track leading out of the right-hand corner. Follow the track along the left-hand edge of a field. Where the track turns right, keep straight on and follow a footpath along power lines, downhill and across a field. At the bottom of the field, cross a stile and track, and keep ahead at a fingerpost into woods. Maintain your direction through the woods, climbing through the trees, and at the far side, keep straight on up an enclosed path across a meadow, to reach a lane.

3 Turn right along the lane for 100 yards, then turn left into the drive for Lower Woodend Farm. Follow the drive to a gate, ignoring turns to the left. Go through the gate and keep straight on along a field, with a fence on your right hand. At the top of the field, ignore a stile on your right but cross a stile directly ahead. Turn half left along the next large field on a grassy track, with a fence on your left, curving left with the fence. After 200 yards turn right at a fingerpost and cross the field to pass through trees onto a footpath. Turn left to a T-junction with a concrete track. Turn left and follow the concrete track past the gates to Squirrel Court and out to a lane, by the gates to Upper Woodend Farm.

4 Turn right along the lane for 350 yards to reach a T-junction. Cross a stile immediately ahead, to the right of a gate, and keep straight on across the field to cross a stile into woods. Follow a path through the trees, curving left and descending. At the bottom of the slope, cross a bridleway and maintain your line of advance up the opposite slope, to a stile into a field. Go ahead up the left-hand side of the field, a fence on your left. About 20 yards short of trees ahead, cross a stile on your left and immediately turn right again, to continue in the same direction, now with the fence on your right, passing the trees on your right.
   Shortly after the trees, cross a stile on your right, back into the original field. Immediately turn left, to again resume your line of advance, now with the fence on your left again. Follow the fence for 50 yards to a stile beside a gate. Cross the stile and keep straight on along a drive to reach a lane.

5 Cross the lane and keep straight on, down a track. Follow the track along the edge of a field and into woods.

These woods were used until the late 1960s for charcoal burning, a traditional industry in the Chilterns.

Just inside the woods, go over a cross-track and keep straight on, descending on a track through the trees. After 300 yards look for a white arrow on a tree to the right of the track. Here leave the track and turn LEFT onto a path into the trees. Follow the path to a kissing gate in a deer fence.

6 Go through the gate and keep straight ahead, on a path through the trees. Follow this white-arrowed path, soon through the trees on the edge of parkland, to emerge into open ground in front of Stonor House.

Stonor Park has been renowned for its venison since deer were introduced here in Tudor times, and there is still a large herd of fallow deer that can occasionally be seen in the grounds.

Keep straight on along a path that winds around the side of the hill across open parkland. Stonor House is seen down to the right.

The first mention of a dwelling on this site was in AD 774, when King Offa of Mercia granted land here to one of his earls, who built a house on the site of a prehistoric stone circle (which has been recreated within the grounds). The present house and chapel were started in 1280 by the first of the Stonor family, Lord Camoy, and were largely completed within 30 years. Over the centuries, the house grew piecemeal as additions and alterations were made, the result being a sprawling structure full of passages, galleries and staircases. The complexity of the structure is increased by the fact that the house is built into the hillside, with the result that rooms that are on the first floor at the front open onto lawns at the rear, and to the rear of the ground floor rooms are subterranean cellars. In the 18th century the red-brick façade seen today was added to the sprawling medieval house.

The interior of Stonor Park, with its maze of nooks and crannies, was put to good use during the reigns of Henry VIII and Elizabeth I. Catholics were regularly hidden by the Stonor family from the officers of the Crown, sometimes ordinary Englishmen fleeing from persecution, sometimes foreign priests sent by the Catholic powers of France and Spain to ferment trouble in England. Several priest-holes are to be seen in Stonor Park, most notable being a cramped cell hidden behind a chimney. It was here that in 1581 the Jesuit Edmund Campion operated a printing press, producing leaflets designed to stir loyal Catholics to mutiny against Queen Elizabeth, including his most famous (or notorious) tract, 'Ten Reasons'.

As well as priest holes, the interior of the house contains a fascinating library, a fine collection of art and tapestries spanning several centuries, and the chapel, built in the 13th century and one of only three Catholic chapels in England to have been in continual use since its construction. There is also a small museum devoted to Edmund Campion and to the history of English Catholicism.

Stonor House is open to the public on Sundays between March and September, Bank Holiday Mondays and also on Wednesdays throughout July and August. Telephone: 01491 638587 for further details.

Follow the path down through the park to a kissing gate leading onto the lane. Turn right for a few yards back to the main gates of Stonor Park.

WALK 10

DONNINGTON CASTLE AND THE ENGLISH CIVIL WAR

Length: 4 miles

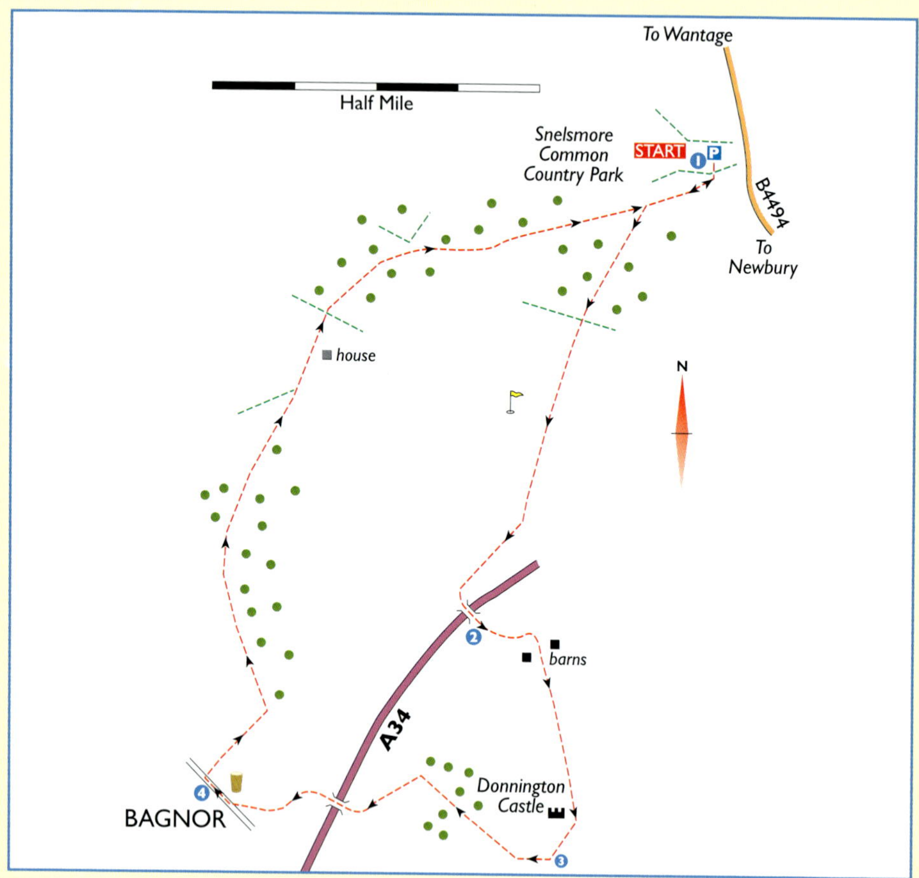

HOW TO GET THERE: The walk starts from Snelsmore Common Country Park, on the B4494 Newbury to Wantage road, 1 mile north of Donnington.

PARKING: There is a large free car park at Snelsmore Common.

MAP: OS Landranger 174 (GR 464710).

INTRODUCTION

This walk starts by crossing the beautiful Snelsmore Common, then goes across open upland with excellent views over the rolling countryside, to reach the ruins of Donnington Castle. The return leg is through attractive open woodland. The walk is mostly off-road, easy underfoot and route-finding is simple. The terrain is undulating, but with no severe slopes.

HISTORICAL BACKGROUND

In 1629 Charles I dissolved Parliament, which had refused to finance the Crown without in turn receiving a voice in the government of the country. For the next 13 years the king's attempts to rule without Parliament led him to impose increasingly draconian methods of raising money. These taxes fell heavily upon the propertied and commercial classes, increasingly alienating the very people who made up the bulk of Parliament's support. Although they made many attempts to negotiate a compromise, their efforts were continually thwarted by the king's intransigence. By 1642 the situation had deteriorated to the point where both sides realized that they must either fight or surrender, and both king and Parliament set about raising troops.

King Charles raised his standard in Nottingham in August 1642. His march on London to seize the capital and end the war at a stroke was thwarted at the battle of Edgehill. Instead the King retreated to Oxford, which became his capital for the remainder of the Civil War. A pattern to the conflict was soon established. Both sides fortified a series of towns and castles with which they could defend areas of the country loyal to themselves; both sides manoeuvred armies around the country, attempting to bring their opponent to battle and impose a decisive defeat, and also to strike at the economic support their opponent controlled.

Inevitably the Midlands saw much action during the Civil War. Not only were the Parliamentarians attempting to capture Charles' capital Oxford, whilst the King was attempting to thrust down the Thames valley to Parliament's main stronghold in London, but for both sides control of the Midlands would have inevitably damaged their opponent's lines of communication.

The castle keep

Donnington Castle was one of a number of Royalist strongholds defending the approaches to Oxford, and Newbury was the location of two major battles during the Civil War. In September 1643 the main Parliamentarian army was marching back to London after raising the siege of Gloucester, and the Royalists intercepted them at Newbury, in a bold attempt to end the war with one decisive battle. Despite a day's heavy fighting, neither side achieved an outright victory at the first battle of Newbury, and the war continued.

For much of 1644 the main actions in the Civil War were in the north and the south-west of England, but by the autumn the conflict had returned to the Midlands. In October 1644 Newbury and Donnington Castle were again in the centre of the fighting, in what became known as the second battle of Newbury.

THE WALK

❶   With your back to the toilet block at the entrance to the car park, walk ahead along the 'Permitted bridle path'. In 20 yards go through a gate, turn right and follow the path, the fence close on your right. In 200 yards, after the end of the car park, fork left at a finger post, signed 'Public bridleway'.

Snelsmore Common was first inhabited by man in the Bronze Age, when large areas of virgin forest were cleared by fire and axe to provide rich agricultural land. The primitive farming methods were unable to sustain the land, however, which eventually deteriorated to an expanse of heath and bog. It was declared common land after the Norman invasion in 1066, and remained such until 1485, when it was given into private ownership under the Tudors. Today Snelsmore Common is an environment unique in southern England, habitat for many rare species of flora and fauna, and protected as a Site of Special Scientific Interest.

At a cross-track keep ahead to reach a metal gate. Go through the gate and follow the path, passing a cottage on your left. Follow the path, soon an enclosed track, past a golf course on your right. The track, eventually tarmacked, bears right and then finally turns left over a bridge across the A34.

❷   Ignore a turn to 'The 9th Tee' but bear left and climb with the track to a bridleway fingerpost. Here turn right, passing an old barn on your left and another barn on your right. Follow the track past cottages and keep ahead to reach Donnington Castle. Turn right through a pedestrian gate to enter the castle.

In the 14th century the manor of Donnington was owned by the Abberbury family, who built a small, unfortified tower on the hill above the town. Richard de Abberbury fought alongside Edward the Black Prince during the Hundred Years War, in gratitude for which Edward's son, King Richard II, gave him permission in 1386 to fortify the tower and create a castle. Donnington Castle was always a compact structure, consisting of a strong gatehouse (the original tower), behind which was built a curtain wall that ran around the top of the hill, the wall itself fortified by two towers. Its history, however, and that of its owners, was eventful.

In 1415 Donnington Castle passed to Thomas Chaucer, son of the poet Geoffrey, and in 1434 it was part of the marriage settlement between Thomas' daughter Alice and William de la Pole, the ambitious Earl of Suffolk whose support and encouragement of Queen Margaret stoked the fires of the Wars of the Roses. William's grandson, John, died at Stoke supporting Lambert Simnel's revolt against Henry VII, and the castle was forfeited to the Crown. Edward VI held privy councils here; Elizabeth I owned the castle and stayed here, before granting it to the Earl of Nottingham.

Donnington Castle first saw action during the Civil War, nearly 300 years after it was built. Its owner John Packer supported Parliament, but its strategic importance on the southern approaches to Oxford was considerable and Charles I seized it in 1642. He garrisoned it with 200 men and four cannon, a huge garrison for such a small castle. The medieval curtain wall was insufficient in the new age of gunpowder, and they were surrounded by extensive earthworks, in a four-star pattern.

Two attempts were made by Parliamentarian forces to take the castle in 1644, both abortive, and the castle was the centre of the second battle of Newbury. After that battle was over and the King's forces retreated, Donnington remained in Royalist hands, and was subjected to the longest siege of the Civil War, nearly two years. Finally, in 1646, Parliamentarian forces under Colonel Parker succeeded in battering down large sections of the walls with mortars and, after heavy fighting, the Royalist Captain Donne negotiated an honourable surrender, marching his garrison, still armed, from the ruins of the castle, to join the Royalists at Wallingford. The castle was further destroyed to render it unusable ever again.

From the castle keep, follow the footpath down the slope to the car park.

Look down onto the river plain below you. Just below the castle is the river Lambourn, beyond that the settlement of Speen, today a suburb of Newbury, and beyond that, lost in the conurbation, the river Kennet. In 1644 there was only a tiny hamlet at Speen, surrounded by fields and meadows, astride the main Bristol-London road. It was here, between the two rivers, that the second battle of Newbury was fought on 27 October 1644. The Parliamentarian army of 19,000 men was advancing from your left, behind the sprawl of modern north Newbury, whilst the Royalists, 10,000 strong, were advancing from your right. Although the Parliamentarian army was spotted by the garrison at Donnington, King Charles was taken by surprise. He hastily drew up his army in front of where you are standing, the main force roughly where the Newbury by-pass now runs, the advance guard immediately below you. There was heavy fighting off to your left, around the present Shaw school, with confusing attacks and counter-attacks lasting until nightfall. When darkness fell, both sides believed they had lost the battle.

Under cover of darkness, King Charles retreated towards Oxford, leaving the garrison in Donnington Castle to its fate.

3 Turn right through the car park and pass between concrete bollards onto a footpath, the fence around the castle close on your right.

REFRESHMENTS

The Blackbird public house is passed halfway around the walk. It offers a good range of food and ales, and has a very pleasant beer garden. Telephone: 01635 40638.

Look up to your right for good views of the earthworks raised by the Royalist garrison. They surmount the top of the hill and also the false summit below it, and offered an excellent first line of defence in front of the strong medieval curtain wall.

Keep ahead along a path through woodland, to reach a stile leading onto a concrete drive. Turn left, immediately crossing a second drive and keep ahead down a footpath, through a tunnel of hedges. Join the drive and keep ahead over a bridge, again crossing the A34.

Below and to the left was where the bulk of the Royalist army was drawn up for the second battle of Newbury.

At the end of the bridge turn left at a fingerpost and go down a tarmac path. At the bottom, go through a kissing gate and bear right along a gravel drive to reach a lane at the Blackbird public house.

4 Pass the Blackbird on your right and maintain your former direction along the lane for 50 yards, and then turn right onto a footpath between houses. Go through a kissing gate and keep ahead up the field, following waymark posts. At the top of the field go through a kissing gate and turn left to follow a path through the edge of woods. Continue along the tree-lined path for ½ mile to join a drive.

Keep ahead along the drive. Pass a house on the right and climb to a kissing gate into woods. Keep ahead (the left-most path), soon with a fence on the left. Where the fence ends keep ahead, climbing steadily. At the top of the slope, at a cross-track, turn right along a broad track. Keep to the main waymarked track, ignoring side turns, eventually crossing a tarmac path. Keep ahead along a gravel path, in 100 yards reaching the car park. Keep ahead, fence on your left, back to the start.

WALK 11

BURFORD AND THE END OF THE LEVELLERS (1649)

Length: 5 miles

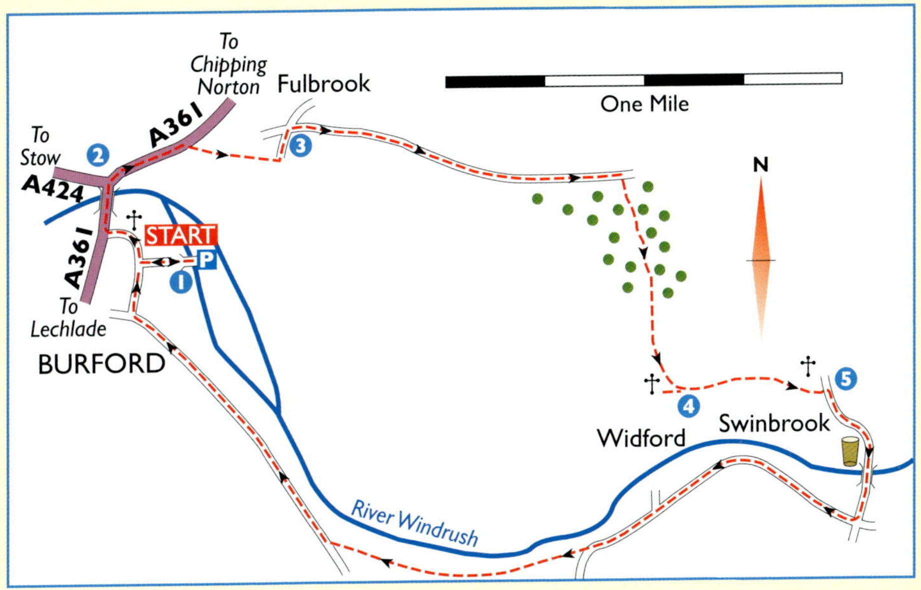

HOW TO GET THERE: The walk starts from the car park in the centre of Burford, on the A40, 24 miles west of Oxford and the same distance east of Cheltenham.

PARKING: The free car park is signposted, at the northern end of the High Street, behind the church.

MAP: OS Landranger 163 (GR 254124).

INTRODUCTION

Picturesque Burford makes a fine setting for this fascinating walk and its honey-coloured houses and old coaching inns are an attractive backdrop to the dramatic story of the Levellers. The route heads out through woods and meadows to visit two historic churches and the site of a village destroyed by the Black Death, before returning along a quiet lane and footpath beside the river Windrush.

HISTORICAL BACKGROUND

In 1649, although the king was dead and the Civil War effectively over, England remained in a state of political turmoil. Government was in the hands of only 60 or so MPs, radical Independents who had survived the purging of Parliament by Colonel Pride and who now held power only with the army's support. Although this Parliament passed a number of republican reforms, power still firmly rested with the landed gentry. This was deeply resented by the Levellers, a group representing the lower middle classes, who had fought against the king to reform society and now saw themselves as still excluded from any share in the body politic.

Leveller influence was particularly strong within the army. Not only had the army become politicised during the war, but its soldiers were very angry about pay being many months in arrears, and deeply unhappy at the prospect of being sent to Ireland to fight against rebels there. In the spring of 1649 pamphlets written by the Leveller leader John Lilburne were openly distributed and widely read amongst soldiers, and stirred the army up into demands for political reform and the settling of grievances. In London the rejection of a Leveller petition to Parliament demanding poor relief provoked a riot by apprentices and shopkeepers, and troops sent to suppress the riot instead joined it. The mutiny was rapidly and firmly put down by troops loyal to Parliament. The leader of the uprising, Robert Lockyer, was executed, creating a martyr whose death added further to discontent within the army.

In the face of continued unsettled grievances and under pressure from Leveller agitation, more soldiers deserted, and in May 1649 started to congregate in the vicinity of Banbury before marching towards Oxford. Denied access to the city, some 1,200 disaffected soldiers marched westwards towards Bristol, their numbers swelling as they went. They were shadowed by a force led by Cromwell and Sir Thomas Fairfax, determined to suppress what they saw as mutiny. On 13 May 1649 the deserters reached the town of Burford and camped for the night, where they opened negotiations with Fairfax about their demands.

Burford church

THE WALK

1 Leave the car park, cross the river and keep ahead to walk back along Church Lane. Bear right with the lane to the church.

Burford church was where the Leveller dream ended. The Levellers were so convinced that General Fairfax would leave them in peace whilst negotiations were underway that they posted few pickets and scattered amongst the houses and inns of Burford to sleep for the night. In the small hours Fairfax's cavalry, led by Colonel John Reynolds, himself once a Leveller sympathiser, rushed the town. A few men fired their pistols but resistance was over before it began. Over 800 mutineers melted away into the night, but 340 were arrested and imprisoned in the church. One Leveller, Anthony Sedgely, carved his name into the lead rim of the font, where it can still be seen today.

The Levellers failed at first to realise the seriousness of their situation, and repeated their demands for back pay, a wider franchise and a say in army policy. Fairfax curtly refused to listen, and informed the Levellers that they all faced the death penalty for mutiny. In the face of this, the mutineers promised to resume their loyalty to Parliament and begged for mercy. This had been Fairfax's objective all along, and he court-martialled just four of the mutineers as an object lesson. Those chosen were men who had stuck to their beliefs, and significantly were not officers but lower ranks, two cornets (junior lieutenants) Thompson and Denne, and two corporals Perkins and Church. On 17th May the four were marched into the churchyard to face a firing squad, their former colleagues being ordered onto the church roof to witness the event.

Thompson, Perkins and Church were executed. Denne, a former Baptist minister, repented enthusiastically, claimed he no longer wished to live, produced a winding sheet he had bought to be interred in, and launched into a long tract pointing out his errors to his fellow malcontents. Fairfax reprieved him, and Denne mounted the pulpit to preach at length on the sins of mutiny to his astonished colleagues.

Cromwell also took the opportunity to mount the pulpit and assure the mutineers that Providence had spared their lives and their grievances would be addressed. A few days later the last of the Levellers were dispersed near Wellingborough, and the Levellers' dream of widening the gains of the revolution was destroyed.

After visiting the church, continue along Church Lane to the High Street.

Until around 1500 Burford was a major commercial centre, standing on an important ford over the river Windrush, as its church and many fine buildings testify. In 1100 it was granted a charter to hold a weekly market, and this formed the basis of future prosperity. With the growth in the importance of Cotswolds wool, Burford became a centre for the woollen trade, but it was not exclusively a 'wool town', and wool was never its main source of income.

Stone from nearby Taynton, a warm, golden sandstone, was particularly famous as a building material, and was exported throughout England, as well as being used in the town itself. Burford stone was used in Windsor Castle, Eton College and also in nearby Oxford, as well as to build Blenheim Palace (see Walk 14). There still exist many of the fine houses built by wealthy merchants, and also numerous coaching inns that accommodated visitors engaged in trade. The high street contains particularly fine examples. By 1600 Burford was ceasing to be a major commercial centre, but it remained an important waystation on the long-distance coach routes, with up to 30 coaches a day passing through the town in the 17th and 18th centuries, as the many coaching inns still in existence testify.

Turn right along the High Street and follow the road over the river Windrush.

② Continue along the road to a roundabout, then turn right, signed 'A361 Chipping Norton'. In 300 yards pass Walnut Row on the right, and 20 yards later, just past the end of Cotland House B&B, turn right down a drive. In 10 yards, turn left along a gravel drive and 15 yards later, at a gateway, cross a stile to the right of the gate. Follow an enclosed path through a kissing gate and along the side of a paddock to enter a field via a barrier. Keep ahead along the side of the field, a fence on your left. Cross a stile and keep ahead along a second field, to cross a stile in the left corner. Follow an enclosed path to a lane and on to the war memorial in the centre of Fulbrook.

③ Turn right at the war memorial and follow the main road for 80 yards, then turn right down a single-track lane, signed 'Swinbrook'. Follow the lane for ¾ mile, climbing to the top of the ridge and then descending, past woods on the right. In a dip at the far end of the woods, ignore a bridleway on the right, signed 'Widford', but turn right at a footpath 20 yards later, also signed 'Widford'. Descend into a green valley between woods and follow this beautiful winding valley for nearly ½ mile to a gate into a field. Keep straight on across the field to meet a farm track, in front of a telegraph pole.

   Widford church is well worth seeing. Turn right and go through a gate and over a cattle grid, then immediately turn right to the church on the slope on your right.

The church of St Oswald here at Widford was built upon the remains of a Roman villa, in or after AD 660, when the body of Oswald, King of Northumbria, rested here on its way to Lindisfarne following the king's death in battle against the Mercians. A Saxon village grew up around the church, and prospered until 1348, when the Black Death decimated the population. The undulations in the fields around the church are the remains of that village. On the wall of the church there are still murals, dating from 1350, painted after the Black Death to give a cautionary message regarding the transience of life. Thirteen households survived the Black Death, but by 1500 only three remained.

4 After visiting the church, return to the track and turn left through the gate again. Aim for a white post to the left of the cottage ahead. Continue ahead, the cottage fence on your right, and where the fence ends, keep straight on to a gate on the far side of the field. Cross a stile by the gate and go half right down the next field to a gate in the wall on the far side. Go through the gate and along an enclosed path. At the end turn left and go through a white gate ahead into Swinbrook churchyard. Follow the path past the church door.

The church of St Mary dates from around 1200, and was mostly added to until the 15th century. The nave is from the original Norman period, with Early English additions; the chancel is 13th-century Perpendicular; while the aisle and east window date from the 15th century. The tower was an afterthought, raised in six weeks in 1822.

Swinbrook was the seat of the Fettiplace family, important landowners who held the manor of Swinbrook. They came to power under Henry VII, whose squire was Anthony Fettiplace. The family prospered in Tudor times, with the growth of the woollen industry. Their manor house was just to the south of the church, and was the finest Tudor house in Oxfordshire, but today nothing remains of it. The family spent a lot of money beautifying the church, and there are two sets of magnificent effigies in the church: one set, late Tudor in design, was commissioned from a local mason by Sir Edmund Fettiplace, grandson of Anthony, and is of Sir Edmund, his father, and grandfather: the second, finer set was the work of sculptor William Bird of Oxford, and undertaken in 1686 to portray three of Sir Edmund's descendants, in a more realistic, late Stuart, style. The grave of Nancy Mitford, the 20th-century novelist, is in the churchyard.

5 Follow the path through the churchyard. Do not fork left but keep ahead to a gate and steps leading down to the street. Turn right through the village of Swinbrook to the Swan public house and cross the bridge over the river Windrush. Keep ahead to a crossroads. Turn right, signed 'Widford and Burford', and walk along this quiet lane for ½ mile to Widford.

In the hamlet of Widford, pass a side road, signed 'No through road', on your right. Continue along the road for 200 yards. Where the road bends left, take a path beside a gate on the right and follow it down to the river. Keep ahead along the riverside for ¾ mile, crossing stiles at intervals. The path eventually returns to the road. Cross a stile and turn right. Follow the road, soon on a roadside path, into Burford. Opposite the Royal Oak public house, turn right down Guildenford, and then turn right back to the car park.

ASHDOWN HOUSE AND THE WINTER QUEEN

Length: 5½ miles

Ashdown House

HOW TO GET THERE: The walk starts from outside the Rose and Crown public house in Ashbury, which is on the B4000, 3 miles south of Shrivenham.

PARKING: There is ample roadside parking in the village, but please park with consideration for residents.

MAP: OS Landranger 174 (GR 265850).

INTRODUCTION

Ashdown House is forever associated with Elizabeth of Bohemia, known to history as the 'Winter Queen'. This walk starts in the village of Ashbury, climbs onto the downs and then descends to Ashdown House, approaching it along a magnificent formal 'ride' through woodland, before returning across the downs. The walk is almost entirely on tracks and footpaths, with two gradual ascents and descents. Route-finding is easy and the terrain is good underfoot.

HISTORICAL BACKGROUND

In 1613 King James I arranged the marriage of his daughter Elizabeth to Frederick V, the Elector Palatine, a German prince short of land but politically powerful. The marriage cemented England's relations with the Protestant powers of northern Europe. Unusually in political marriages, Elizabeth and Frederick, both only 16, rapidly fell in love, and were devoted to each other for the remainder of Frederick's short life. Tragedy soon struck. In 1618, Bohemian Protestants, fearing

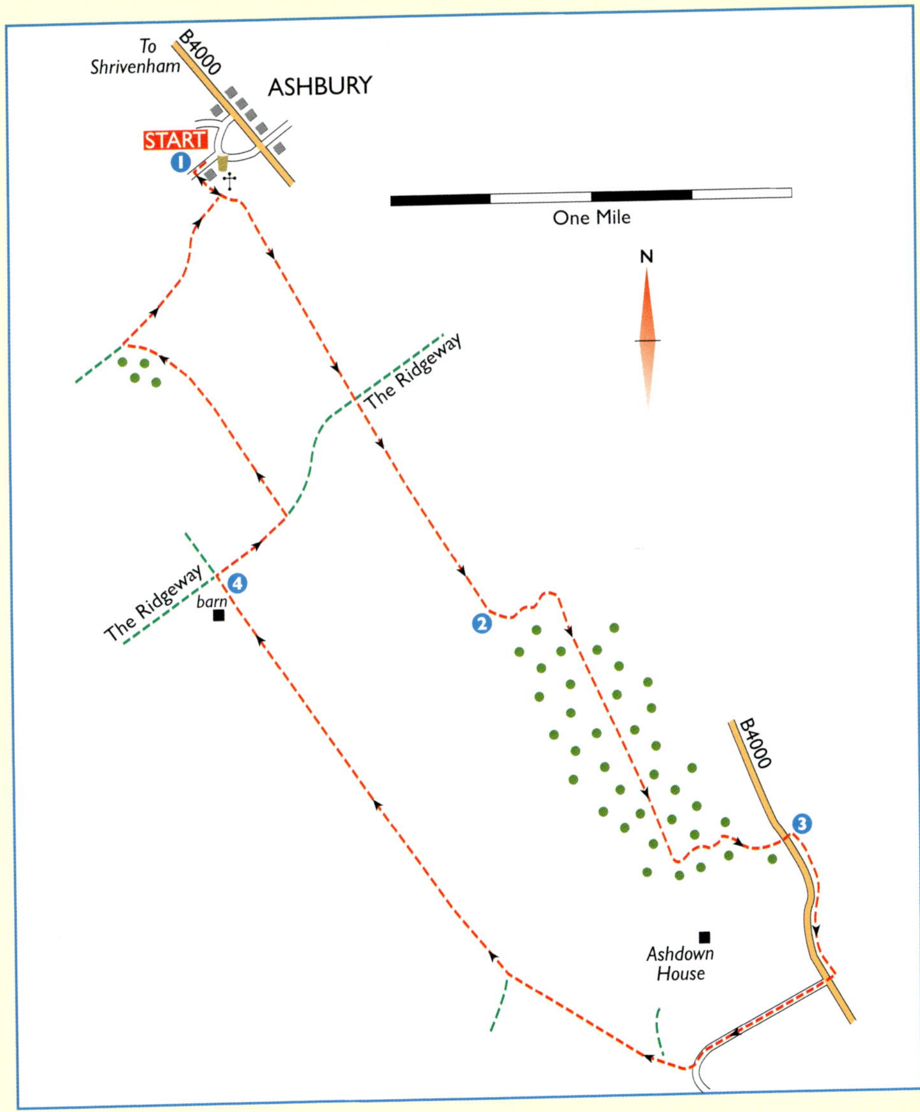

for their safety, rebelled against their Catholic rulers, and offered the crown of Bohemia to Frederick, which he unwisely accepted. Frederick and Elizabeth moved to Prague, and in 1619 were duly crowned King and Queen of Bohemia. But after ruling for only one winter, Frederick was deposed by a Catholic army and forced to flee. The Thirty Years War had begun in Europe and, so too, had Elizabeth's life as an exile.

With central Europe collapsing into turmoil, and the Palatine as well as Bohemia occupied, Frederick was offered sanctuary in Holland by his uncle, Prince Maurice of Nassau. Serving Prince Maurice was a young English soldier of fortune, William, 1st Earl of Craven, who placed his life and his fortune at the service of the 'Winter Monarchs'. When Frederick died in 1632, Craven continued to serve Elizabeth devotedly for the rest of her life.

After Frederick's death, Elizabeth no longer had any political value to Maurice of Nassau, and she appealed unsuccessfully to her brother, Charles I of England, for help. Craven came to her rescue, paying off her mounting debts as well as leading troops in vain attempts to regain her lost kingdom. He raised money for Elizabeth's son, Prince Rupert, to lead an army into Bohemia, and also subsidized Rupert when he came to England in 1642 to fight for his uncle in the English Civil War. This action led Parliament to seize Craven's estates, but he nevertheless continued to give Elizabeth generous financial support.

With the Restoration of the Monarchy in 1660, Elizabeth returned to England, where Craven gave her the use of his London house. Elizabeth died two years later, a penniless exile entirely dependent upon the support of her friends. Craven was her most loyal and devoted friend for 30 years, but despite speculation to the contrary, there is no evidence of any romantic or sexual liaison between them. According to family legend, Craven started building Ashdown House in 1660 as a permanent home for Elizabeth. Although she died in 1662, and never saw the completed house, Ashdown is always associated with the 'Winter Queen'.

THE WALK

❶ Facing the Rose and Crown, go up Church Lane on the right-hand side of the pub and at the top of the lane take the footpath to the right of Churchyard Cottage. Where the path bends right into the overflow graveyard, go left onto a footpath, a fence close on your right. Follow the footpath as it bends left. At a junction, where the main path drops left into a tunnel of trees, turn right at a waymark and follow the path uphill. Follow the footpath for ½ mile to reach a cross-track (the Ridgeway). Cross the Ridgeway and keep ahead along the footpath opposite. Follow this footpath for ½ mile. Pass isolated trees and keep ahead to the corner of a wood.

❷ Where the way ahead is blocked by a fence (a waymarked stile at the right-hand corner) go left into the woods. (This is a permissive path: the public right of way goes down the outside of the woods.) Bear left and follow a clear path along the edge of woodland. Emerge onto a broad cross-track and turn right.

The Ashdown estate consists of approximately 500 acres of woodland, park, downland and pasture. Here, to the north of the house, are two interconnected woods, laid out with meandering rides which lead off from this magnificent avenue. Known as the Northern Ride, this avenue, almost a mile long, led from the house through the woods, and was cut for recreational riding by the owner and his guests. The avenue is narrower at this end than it is nearer the house, a deliberate optical illusion that when seen from the house makes the ride seem even longer.

Follow the broad avenue towards the house, until a chain fence bars further access.

William Craven's father had been Lord Mayor of London under Elizabeth I and, on his death, his widow invested his fortune in land, buying Combe Abbey, Warwickshire in 1610 and Hampstead Marshall, 20 miles from here in Berkshire, in 1618. Seven years later the Ashbury Estate, which included a deer park here at Ashdown, was bought by Lady Craven to provide hunting at a convenient distance from Hampstead Marshall. There was a hunting lodge where the house now stands.

William Craven demolished the hunting lodge and started building Ashdown House sometime after 1660, in his own words 'consecrating it to Elizabeth'. Craven employed one or both of his two regular architects, William Winde and Sir Balthasar Gerbier, to design the house, which is a simple square, each face set to one of the four points of the compass, and each face with a nearly identical façade. It is tall and narrow, more like a town house than a country mansion, with two detached pavilions which acted as kitchens and domestic quarters. Inside, the house is divided into four equal quarters, through one of which runs a magnificent staircase which gives access to all the rooms. The house contains a number of portraits, including the family, Elizabeth of Bohemia and her descendants.

Whether Ashdown House was seriously intended as a country home for Elizabeth of Bohemia is disputed. Certainly she died just after building work started, and the house was still not completed when Lord Craven died in 1697.

Ashdown House is open Wednesday and Saturday afternoons, 2 pm to 5 pm, April to October. There is an admission charge (free to members of the National Trust).

Five yards short of the fence, turn left onto a footpath into the woods. Follow the path as it meanders through open woodland to reach a small unsurfaced car park. Follow the gravel access drive out to the road and turn right for 10 yards, then go left through a kissing gate at a National Trust sign.

3 Walk along the bottom of Kingstone Down, the fence and road close on your right.

There are good views of Ashdown House to your right. The twin pavilions standing in front of the house make the building look far larger from this side.

In ¼ mile, cross a stile on your right. Cross the road and keep ahead along the lane opposite, passing between the entrance gates to Ashdown House on your right and a stable block on the left. Where the lane bends left, keep ahead along a track. Bear right with the track and immediately around the corner, at a fork of tracks, bear left, away from Ashdown House.

In ¼ mile, the track you are on leaves the field and joins another track coming in from the left. Keep ahead. After 1 mile, pass barns on the left and 30 yards later, turn right onto the Ridgeway.

4 Follow the Ridgeway for ¼ mile, then turn left at a fingerpost, onto a clear footpath crossing a field. Follow the footpath downhill. Ignore paths going off left near trees, but keep ahead on the main path, a tree-lined dry valley over to your left, down to a T-junction at a hedge and turn right. In 200 yards, turn left and then immediately right into an enclosed footpath. Maintain your former direction. Cross a track and keep ahead, a chain-link fence on your left, towards the church seen ahead. Go into the churchyard and keep ahead on a concrete path. Follow the path past the church to a lane, and follow the lane downhill back to the start.

Historical footnote: Although in her lifetime she had seen both her husband and her brother lose their crowns, and she herself spent most of her life a powerless political exile, history has seen the importance of Elizabeth. For when Queen Anne of England was dying, Parliament looked anxiously around for a successor who did not belong to the deposed line of James II. The nearest living relative to Anne was her distant cousin Sophia, the daughter of Elizabeth. Sophia, however, died a few weeks before Anne, and so the Crown of England was offered to Sophia's son, who ascended the throne as George I. Elizabeth of Bohemia was thus the matriarch of a royal dynasty that stretches down nearly three centuries to the present Queen.

HUNGERFORD AND THE GLORIOUS REVOLUTION (1688)

Length: 5 miles

The Bear Hotel at Hungerford where William of Orange stayed

HOW TO GET THERE: The walk starts from St Lawrence's church, Hungerford, reached by following the A338 through the middle of Hungerford, turning west at a mini-roundabout just south of the town bridge, and then turning north down Croft Road.

PARKING: There is ample roadside parking near the church, and there are pay-and-display car parks elsewhere in the town.

MAP: OS Landranger 174 (GR 334687).

INTRODUCTION

The walk starts and finishes along a beautiful stretch of the Kennet and Avon canal. It crosses open fields and rolling countryside, ending in the water meadows of the Kennet before returning to Hungerford and passing historic sites connected with the Glorious Revolution, where negotiation between James II and William of Orange resulted in a change of monarch without involving the armies massed nearby. The walk is mainly flat, and route-finding is easy.

HISTORICAL BACKGROUND

In 1688 England faced a major crisis. The Civil War 40 years previously had resulted in the ascendancy of Parliament and the Protestant religion. Upon the restoration of the monarchy the pragmatic Charles II had not tried, overtly at least, to undermine this settlement. His brother and successor James II, however, tried his best to pull power back from Parliament and to re-establish the Catholic faith. James was initially tolerated although his views upon government were intensely disliked. He was, after all, 52 when he came to the throne in 1685 and had two more liberal, Protestant daughters to succeed him. However, in 1688, he produced a male heir, who would be brought up a Catholic and would take precedence over his sisters. Leading Parliamentarians decided that James was too dangerous to be left on the throne, and plotted his removal.

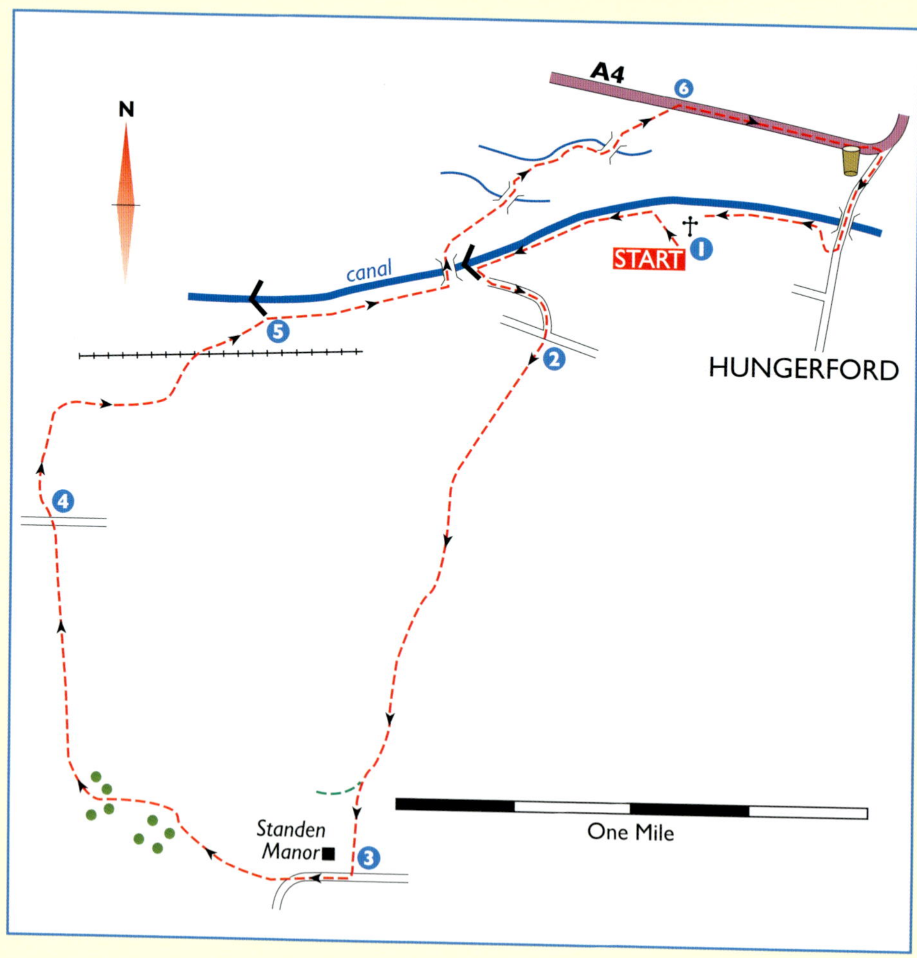

The plotters had a horror of disrupting the social order by unlocking the doors to civil war again. They also knew that a purely internal uprising would not succeed, since James had greatly strengthened the standing army and distributed it to key points in the country. A number of England's most influential men signed an invitation to William, Prince of Orange, leader of the Protestant cause in Europe and husband of James' eldest daughter Mary, to invade England and restore his wife as 'legitimate' heir to the throne. This invitation started what is known to history as the 'Glorious Revolution'.

William, a consummate politician, was anxious to have England a Protestant power, able to threaten the northern frontiers of his main enemy, Catholic France. He saw in the invitation from England's Protestants a major opportunity to further his long-term aims, and accordingly set sail at the head of an army. Instead of landing either in Kent, the obvious point of invasion, or sailing to Yorkshire, already in revolt against King James, William sailed down the Channel and landed at Brixham, in Devon. From there he marched on London, whilst King James made plans to oppose him. The final scene of their conflict was to be played out at Hungerford.

THE WALK

1 Enter the main gates of St Lawrence's churchyard and bear left with a path to the canal tow-path. Turn left along the canal for ½ mile to reach lock gates at Freemans Marsh. At the lock turn sharp left back on yourself, to a path leading to gates between houses. Go through the gate and keep ahead along the quiet lane, eventually passing under a railway arch. Follow the lane to the main road. Cross the main road and go through a gate opposite, at a fingerpost.

2 Keep ahead on a clear path across one field, and then across a second field to reach the corner of a hedge ahead, at a footpath sign. Keep ahead, the hedge now on your left. Follow the path into the field corner and bear right across a stile. Keep ahead on a clear path, climbing gently through new trees to cross a second stile. Follow the path into a field and turn left, to walk along the field edge, the hedge close on your left.

The path eventually becomes a track. Where the track bends right, go left over a stile beside a field gate off to your left. (Warning: the stile is not immediately obvious, and although waymarked, the waymark at the time of writing was obscured by ivy.) Go half right across the field, aiming to the left of two trees that can soon be seen to be standing in mid-field. A fence and wall come into sight on the far side of the field. Aim for a stile, where fence and wall meet.

To your right is Standen Manor. Although the building you see today is largely Victorian, the first manor house was built on this site in the early 12th century, and for three centuries it was the home of the Hussey family. The Hussey line died out and the manor passed in 1486 to Sir Reginald Brey, chief minister to Henry VII, as reward for his support in the toppling of King Richard III the previous year. By the 17th century the house was owned by the Goddard family, who had estates both here and at Bray in the east of the county, where the family had founded almshouses. In 1688, the Goddards' neighbour at Bray was Richard, 3rd Baron Lovelace, who was intimately involved in the plot to replace King James with William of Orange, and it seems likely that the Goddards knew of the scheme. Unlike the earlier occupants of Standen Manor, the Goddards played no active part in this royal toppling, although they swore allegiance to the new monarchs once James had fled into exile.

3   Cross the stile and turn right along the lane, passing a cottage and barn on your left, the manor and cottages on your right. In 350 yards, where the lane turns left, keep ahead at a finger post. Follow the gravel track, barns on your right and a fence on your left. Where the fence ends, keep ahead across a field. Bear right with the track, following telephone lines downhill towards the end of a line of trees ahead. Go around the trees and bear left with the track, still following the telephone lines. On the far side of the field, at a waymark post, keep ahead on a path into woods. Emerge from the trees and follow an enclosed path through new plantations and over a cross-track. Keep ahead along the enclosed footpath. Cross a drive and continue along the enclosed footpath to reach a lane.

4   Cross the lane and continue along the enclosed footpath opposite. In 20 yards, turn right along a track. In ¼ mile, at a junction of tracks, turn right. Follow the track out to a field and turn left. Follow the bottom of the field, the hedge on your left. Where the field boundary meets the railway, go left over a stile and climb steps. Cross the railway with care, descend steps, cross the stile and turn right into a field. Follow the left-hand field boundary, the river Kennet on your left through trees.

5   Opposite a white house on the left, cross a stile onto the canal towpath, and turn right. In ¼ mile, at the next lock gate, cross a footbridge on the left, then go half right across the meadow to a green iron footbridge over the river, 150 yards ahead. Turn left after crossing the bridge, then turn immediately right and go half right across the field, aiming to the left of a double power line pole in mid-field. At the river bank turn right and follow the path, soon crossing the river again. Keep ahead, the main river now on your right, to pass through a kissing gate and then to turn left through a gate on your left to reach a fingerpost. Turn right and follow a clear path, to reach an unmade lane in front of houses.

6   Maintain your direction along the lane to reach a road (the A4). Turn right.

William of Orange had landed at Brixham, Devon, on 5 November 1685, with 11,000 foot soldiers and 4,000 cavalry, the largest disciplined force ever to land in England. The next day the army set off to march to Exeter. The common people turned out to welcome William, many of the local gentry joined him, and on 17 November the Marquis of Bath, commander of the garrison at Plymouth, swore allegiance to William. On 21 November William, his army swollen with volunteers, started to march eastwards, towards London.

By the end of November William's army had advanced along the Kennet valley nearly as far as Hungerford, following the course of the main London-Bristol road (today's A4). Although this was a major road, it was inadequate to provide passage for William's huge force, which was spread out across the countryside, advancing piecemeal along all passable parallel roads.

To oppose William, King James had an army of 34,000 men, vastly larger than that of the invader, encamped near Salisbury and awaiting their king to come and lead them. But James was increasingly aware of the depth of loathing many of his subjects felt for him. Leading noblemen had raised rebellions in Cheshire, Nottingham and York. James' second daughter, Anne, had fled to the rebels, and his chief military commander, John Churchill, declared his allegiance to William. By the time King James joined his army he realized his cause was lost. On 28 November he accepted the advice of his nobles that he should negotiate with William.

Follow the A4 past the Sun Inn to a mini roundabout at the Bear Hotel.

William with his army was a few miles west of Hungerford when news that King James wished to negotiate reached him. The disparate units of the invading army came together and camped in the fields and meadows around the town. William lodged in the Bear Inn, a 13th-century coaching inn on the main London to Bristol road, and the most luxurious accommodation in Hungerford. Here, on 7 December 1685, William met with three commissioners sent from King James to negotiate. William was remarkably conciliatory. He demanded that the king dismiss all Catholics from his service and revoke the proclamations issued against William and his supporters. He also demanded that the king pay the wages of his, William's, army. In return, William would advance no closer to London, on condition James withdrew his forces from the capital also. Both James and William would attend the next session of Parliament, when the limits of royal power and the succession would be decided.

William appeared willing to compromise and even to leave James on his throne, albeit with much reduced power. The king, however, was in no mood for compromise: he had already sent his wife and son to France, and on 11 December he slipped away from London to join them, throwing the Great Seal of England, the monarch's official stamp, into the Thames on his way out as a final act of spite. William had effectively conquered England without firing a shot, and always maintained that he had come to save the nation from tyranny. Despite being pressed by a number of his supporters to take the

Crown for himself, William, ever the shrewd politician and not wishing to be seen as a foreign invader, refused to do so. Instead, he argued that it should legitimately pass to James' oldest daughter, Mary. William did, however, refuse to be merely his wife's consort, but instead let it be known that the Crown should be offered jointly to both his wife and himself, with himself having the right to be king for life, even if Mary died before him. So it was that on 11 April 1686 William and Mary were crowned as England's only joint sovereigns.

REFRESHMENTS

There are numerous pubs and tea-rooms in Hungerford.

Turn right to the town centre and follow the road past the John O'Gaunt Inn to cross the canal.

In 1362 the manor of Hungerford was given to John O'Gaunt, Duke of Lancaster, by his father King Edward III, the beginning of a long association between the town and its new lord.

On the far side of the canal bridge, turn sharp right down to the canal bank. Turn left along the towpath for ¼ mile to reach St Lawrence's church again.

There has been a church dedicated to St Lawrence on this site since the 13th century. The church was almost totally rebuilt in 1816, and has remained largely unaltered since then. The church that William of Orange would have seen has completely disappeared.

BLENHEIM PALACE: HEYDAY OF THE FIRST CHURCHILLS (1704–1710)

Length: 5 miles

Blenheim Palace seen from the Great Lake

HOW TO GET THERE: The walk starts from the car park in Woodstock, on the A44, 6 miles north-west of Oxford.

PARKING: The free car park is at the southern end of the town, clearly signposted to the right just as the town is entered from the Oxford direction.

MAP: OS Landranger 164 (GR 447168).

INTRODUCTION

For most of its route this easy walk is within the grounds of Blenheim Park, with fine views of the palace and lake, but it starts and ends in the attractive town of Woodstock, once a flourishing coaching town on the first turnpike road in Oxfordshire.

HISTORICAL BACKGROUND

John Churchill was born in Devon in 1650, the son of a Royalist squire who had been impoverished during the Civil War. Churchill became a page to James, Duke of York, and through his patronage entered the army in 1667. He remained in James's service, undertaking confidential missions for him, and when in 1685 James became king, Churchill was rewarded with a peerage. As leader of King James's army, Churchill defeated the rebellion led by the Duke of Monmouth, but in 1688 he turned against his lifelong patron and supported William of Orange in his bid for the English throne. He was rewarded with an earldom.

King William, not surprisingly, never really trusted Churchill, who, in turn, remained in secret communication with the exiled James. The devoted friendship

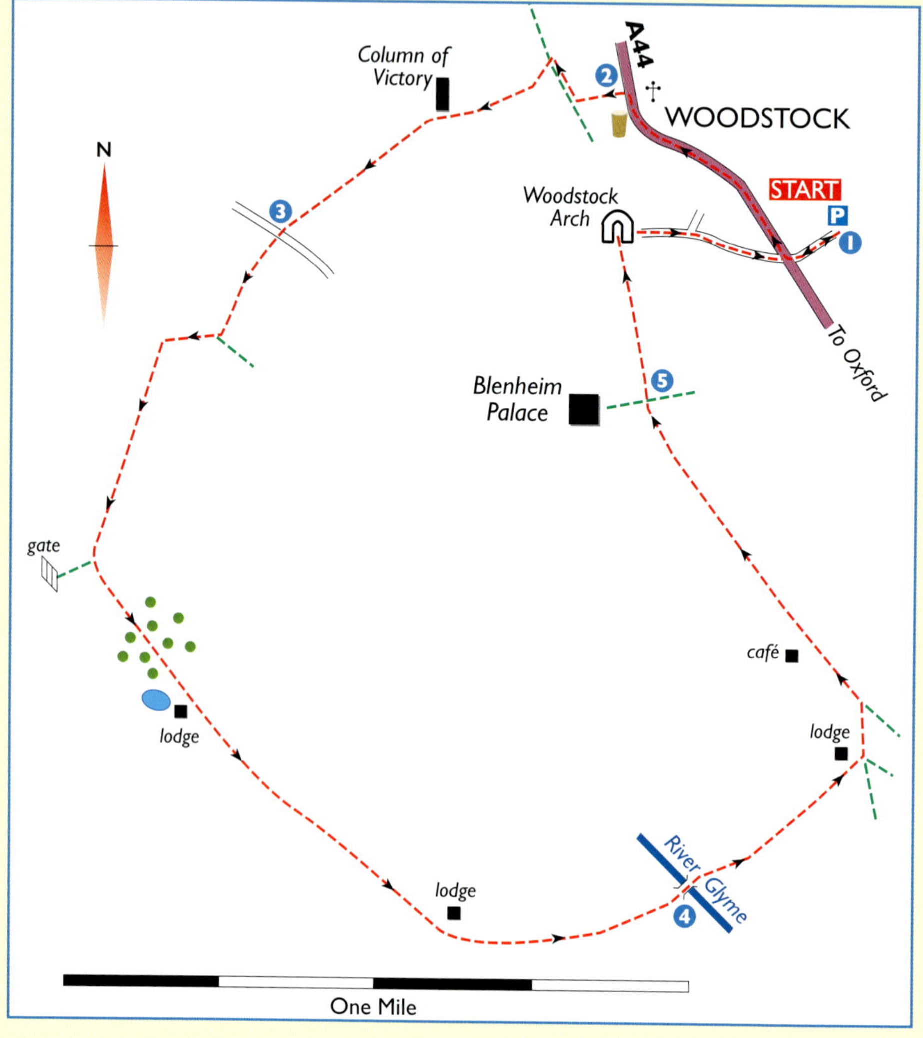

of Princess Anne for Churchill's wife, Lady Sarah, protected Churchill, finally reconciling the king to him. In 1702 William died, Anne became queen, and the heyday of the Churchills arrived: Sir John became Duke of Marlborough and Commander of the Army, Sarah the effective controller of the Queen's official household. Between 1704 and 1709 Marlborough led an Anglo-Dutch army in a series of brilliant victories against the French. The grateful queen gave him the royal estates of Woodstock as a reward, and there built for him a magnificent palace, named Blenheim after his first victory.

But by 1709 the Marlboroughs were increasingly unpopular. The Duke was accused by Parliament of prolonging the war for his own glory, and Sarah's domineering attitude towards the Queen led to a series of bitter rows, culminating in her dismissal from Anne's service in 1711. With the withdrawal of the Queen's patronage Marlborough's days were numbered: he was dismissed from office, his only political ally, his brother-in-law the Earl of Godolphin, died, and in 1712 he left England. Although he returned when Anne died in 1715, he never again saw public office, and retired to Blenheim Palace, where he died in 1722. His pugnacious duchess lived on for another 22 years, engaging in a series of deadly quarrels with all and sundry.

Marlborough has claim to being England's greatest ever general. He was a brilliant and humane commander, and a very dignified and gracious man. He also did not allow scruple to interfere with business, and from this apparent contradiction stemmed his ability to arouse both adoration and deep dislike in those around him.

THE WALK

1 Leave the car park by the exit and turn right along Hessington Road. Pass Union Street and continue to the main road (A44). Turn right and follow the main road through Woodstock.

On your right you pass the George Inn, a coaching inn since at least 1469. Woodstock was on the main coach road between Oxford and the Cotswold wool towns such as Chipping Norton. This was the first turnpike road in Oxfordshire, and one of the first in England, opened in 1718.

Follow the A44 as it bends left and goes downhill.

The Column of Victory can be seen ahead, standing at a high point in Blenheim Park and dominating the landscape for miles around.

Pass the Black Prince public house and ascend with the main road. In 100 yards, at a church on the right, turn left from the road and go past a row of cottages to a wooden kissing gate leading into Blenheim Park.

②   Bear left, soon on a stony footpath, and descend towards the lake.

There is a fine view of Blenheim Palace and park from here. This park was originally part of the royal manor of Woodstock, a hunting estate for the monarchy from Norman times onwards. Henry I built a manor house here in the 12th century, and for the first century of Norman rule Woodstock was the political and economic centre of Oxfordshire. Edward, the Black Prince was born at Woodstock in 1330. Two hundred years later, the future Elizabeth I was imprisoned here during the reign of her sister Mary. The manor was given to John Churchill, 1st Duke of Marlborough, as a reward for his victory at Blenheim in 1704, and Queen Anne paid for a palace to be built. The palace was designed by Sir John Vanbrugh and set in 2,100 acres of parkland, which was later landscaped by 'Capability' Brown.
   The park is open 9 am to 4.45 pm throughout the year.

Turn right along a metalled track. After 200 yards, at a T-junction just past a cottage on the left, turn sharp left onto another metalled path. Follow this path for 200 yards. Cross a stile on your right and keep straight on across the park to the Column of Victory, in sight ahead.

The Column of Victory, with a toga-clad statue of the Duke on top of it, gives the details of Marlborough's famous victories. The Dutchman William III had taken the English throne in part because he needed the resources of England for Holland's ongoing struggle against France and Spain. Queen Anne had inherited this war and sent Marlborough to the Continent as commander of a combined Anglo-Dutch force. The Duke's job was made extremely difficult by the necessity to hold together a political alliance with the Dutch, who were contributing the bulk of the army, and who were reluctant to involve their troops in strategic war aims that were wider than the simple defence of Holland. Between 1704 and 1709 Marlborough fought only four major battles – Blenheim, Ramillies, Oudenarde and Malplaquet – but battles of such genius that his reputation was assured.

From the Column, bear slightly left across the open park to the corner of a fence (Blenheim Palace is directly left of you). Maintain the same line of advance, keeping the fence on your right. Where the fence turns right, keep straight on to reach a drive at a stile.

③   Cross the stile and drive, cross a second stile on the opposite side of the drive, and follow the path opposite down through trees. At a T-junction at the bottom of the slope, turn right for 50 yards to cross a stile over the fence on the left. Turn right along a grassy track, gently climbing the bank and turning left to reach a tarmac drive. Turn left along the drive for ½ mile, to a junction. Do not turn right to the gate but continue along the drive.

You are walking through ancient trees which were here in the days before the park was landscaped. They are survivors of the royal hunting forest of the Norman kings.

Pass a pond and a lodge on the right. Continue along the drive for another ½ mile, passing another lodge on the left and soon thereafter following the drive along the left-hand side of an open meadow. Follow the drive down to a stone bridge over the river Glyme.

The 2,100 acre parkland with its avenues of trees was designed around 1760 by Lancelot 'Capability' Brown, the foremost landscape designer of his day. It was the fashion in the mid-18th century to sculpture parks and gardens to create a 'natural' look that was tidy and aesthetically pleasing, and Brown was the foremost exponent of this art. It is said that the stands and avenues of trees were laid out to represent the disposition of the Duke's troops at Marlborough. Whether there is any truth in this or not, Blenheim Park, with its imaginative use of woods, lakes and rolling open vistas, remains one of Brown's finest creations.

4 Cross the bridge and continue up the drive, crossing an entrance drive to Blenheim Palace on your left. Continue to reach a junction of drives in front of another small lodge. Keep ahead over a cattle grid and continue along the drive for 200 yards to a T-junction. Turn left and follow the drive past a parking area, tea room and adventure playground on your left. Continue along the drive, eventually passing through white gates. Blenheim Palace is on your left.

Blenheim Palace is one of the finest examples of English Baroque architecture in England, and took nearly 20 years to build. As well as donating the estate to Marlborough, Queen Anne also funded the building of a great stately home. Sir John Vanbrugh, soldier, playwright, architect and a member of Marlborough's political and social circle, was chosen by the Duke to design the building. Vanbrugh ignored detailed suggestions given by Sir Christopher Wren, the doyen of English architecture, and created what is undoubtedly his finest work. His progress was plagued by disputes with the Duchess, over his designs and over getting paid for his work, especially after Crown funding ceased in 1711. In 1716 Vanbrugh resigned as architect amidst a welter of law suits, and the work on the palace was finalised by his friend and mentor, Nicholas Hawksmoor.

The palace itself covers 7 acres and is built of golden sandstone from Taynton, near Burford. Inside is a huge collection of tapestries, sculpture, paintings and furniture, set in gilded state rooms. The Long Library, 183 ft in length, is one of the longest rooms in a private house in England and contains over 10,000 books. The Great Hall has elaborate carvings by the stonemason Grinling Gibbons, and a vast painted ceiling by Sir James Thornhill depicting the battle of Blenheim, which rivals in size the artist's own work in Greenwich Hospital. There is an exhibition on the life of Sir

Winston Churchill, grandson to the 8th Duke, based around the rooms where he was born and raised, including a magnificent collection of model soldiers. There is also a private chapel, the centrepiece of which is a monument by Rysbrack to the Duke and Duchess; although at his death in 1722 the Duke was buried in Westminster Abbey, his body was later removed and brought back to Blenheim for re-interment.

The many formal gardens around the house include water terraces, an Italian garden, a rose garden, an arboretum and a cascade, and also the world's largest hedge maze.

Blenheim Palace is open 10.30 am to 5.30 pm, mid-March until the end of October. Guided tours are available if desired. There is an admission charge.

REFRESHMENTS

The Black Prince public house, passed on the route, is an olde worlde pub with a riverside beer garden that offers a good range of food and beers. Telephone: 01993 811530.

5   To continue the walk, go over the cross drive, the palace on your left and parking area on your right, and keep ahead along the drive towards Woodstock Arch.

The Grand Bridge seen on the left spanning the lake epitomised the disputes between Vanbrugh and the Duchess of Marlborough. To Vanbrugh, it was a fine finishing touch, and provided a foreground to the baroque splendour of the palace: he called it a 'castle in the air'. To the Duchess it was grandiose, tasteless and extravagant.

Woodstock Arch was one of the last parts of Blenheim Palace to be completed. By 1722 relations between the Duchess and Vanbrugh had deteriorated so far that they were suing one another. Vanbrugh was dismissed and Nicholas Hawksmoor, Vanbrugh's mentor, was brought in to complete the work. The Woodstock Arch is Hawksmoor's own individual contribution to Blenheim.

Go through the arch and turn right along the road (Park Street), passing Georgian houses on the left and soon some old stocks. Fork right in front of the Municipal Building and go along Market Place. Follow the left-hand pavement, which at the end of Market Place becomes an enclosed alley leading to the A44. Cross the A44 at pedestrian lights. Turn right for 10 yards, then turn left into Hessington Road and back to the car park.

WALK 15

WROXTON ABBEY AND THE AMERICAN WAR OF INDEPENDENCE (1756)

Length: 4 miles

Wroxton Tower

HOW TO GET THERE: The walk starts at the village pond in the centre of Wroxton, on the A422, 2 miles west of Banbury. Three side roads lead south off the A422 into Wroxton, all meeting at the pond.

PARKING: There is ample roadside parking around the pond and surrounding green.

MAP: OS Landranger 151 (GR 415418).

INTRODUCTION

From Wroxton's village pond the walk goes out over rolling countryside and through woodland, on field paths and quiet lanes. On the way enjoy fine views of Wroxton Abbey and its gardens, to return to visit the ancient church where both Lord North and Sir William Pope, builder of Wroxton Abbey, lie buried.

HISTORICAL BACKGROUND

In the century before 1770 Britain's colonial policy was based on simple economic assumptions: the colonies were there to provide the raw materials needed for British industry and trade, and to buy the surpluses of British manufacturers. This was resented by colonists, particularly in the Americas, who had a sturdy mercantile tradition of their own. Legislation in Parliament from the time of the Commonwealth onwards implemented this policy and increased colonial resentment. It was against this background that Lord North of Wroxton became prime minister.

Frederick, Lord North, was born in 1732 and grew up partly on the family estate at Wroxton. In 1754 he entered parliament as MP for the 'rotten borough' of Banbury, a seat where the few electors were tenants of the Norths and who voted as the family instructed. By 1767 he had become First Lord of the Treasury and Leader of the House of Commons, in practice 'prime minister' (North never used that title himself, pedantically but rightly stating that there was 'no such thing

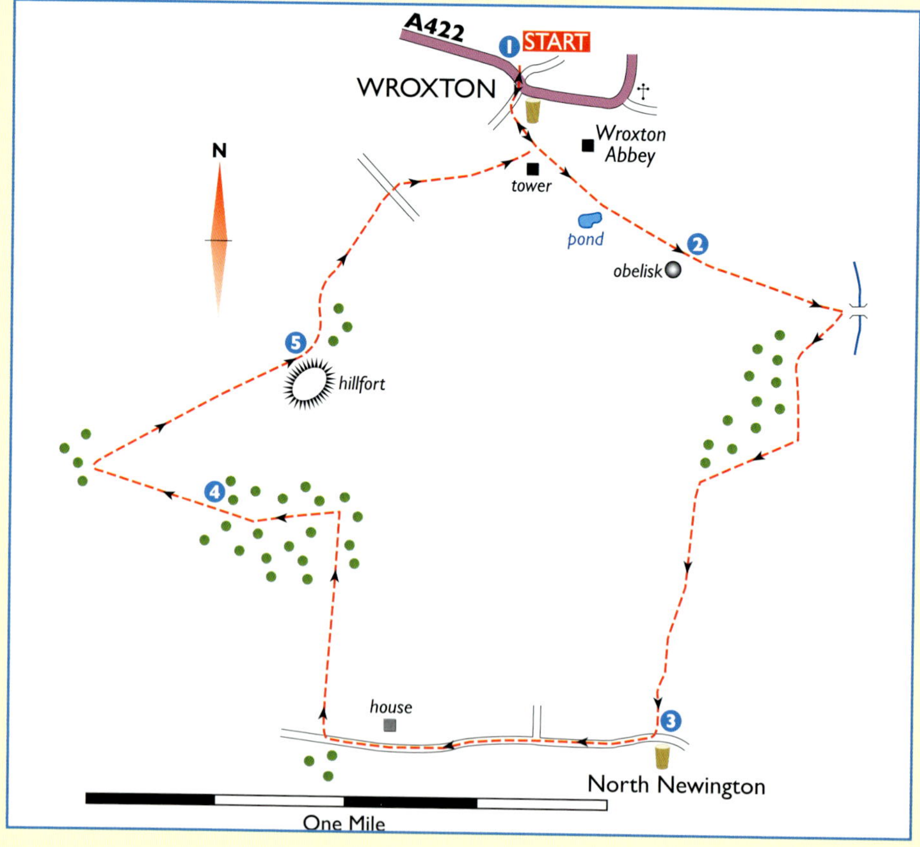

under the British Constitution'). At the time the parliamentary institutions we know today were in their infancy. The political parties did not have any rigid adhesion but were more a collection of personal loyalties tied to individual leaders; the king had not yet fully relinquished power to Parliament; ministers were not formally makers of policy. The easy-going North saw himself as the agent of the king, not his advisor, and it was George III who dictated policy.

North, unlike the king and the rest of his councillors, recognised the Americans' grievances and gave them a number of tax concessions. He failed, however, to repeal Tea Duty, which caused the colonies to pay taxes on English goods they did not want and, in 1773, colonists threw a cargo of tea into Boston Harbour. North made further concessions, despite the king's opposition, but failed to appease and in 1776 the American War of Independence began. North's attempt to resign was not accepted, and he struggled on for a further five years before finally resigning in 1782, against the king's wishes.

North soon became the scapegoat for both king and press for the loss of the American colonies. His personal support in Parliament dwindled, his eyesight failed, and in 1790, now Lord Guildford, he retired from politics. His last years were divided between London and his Wroxton estate. He died in 1792 and was buried in Wroxton church.

THE WALK

① Standing with your back to the pond, walk across the road towards the gates of Wroxton College, formerly Wroxton Abbey, and go up the lane (Dark Lane) to the right of the gates. After 80 yards turn left at a footpath sign, marked 'Banbury', and go down an enclosed footpath between a house and the grounds of Wroxton Abbey. Go through a kissing gate into a field. Keep ahead, with the fence on your left.

The present house of Wroxton Abbey can be seen to the left, while to the right is a solitary tower, all that remains of the original Abbey (the tower is passed at the end of the walk). There was an Augustinian priory on this site from 1217 until the Dissolution of the Monasteries in 1536, when the property was bought by Sir Thomas Pope. Pope founded Trinity College, Oxford and gave the abbey to the college, but stipulated that his brother John and his heirs would have the right of tenancy. The present house was built in 1618 by one of those heirs, Sir William Pope, later created 1st Earl of Downe, on the site of the former priory, and called 'Wroxton Abbey'. It has an impressive four-storey central porch, flanked by gabled bay windows. The interior has a plethora of carved wood, a fine example of Jacobean interior design. In the late 17th century the house passed through marriage to Sir Francis North, Lord Guildford, who served Charles II as Keeper of the Great Seal of England. It remained until 1932 in the North family.

It is perhaps ironic that in 1963 the Abbey was sold to the Fairleigh Dickinson University of New Jersey, USA, and is today used by them as a residential college.

Bear right away from the fence to a kissing gate beside a field gate, behind trees. Go through the gate and turn three-quarters left downhill. Soon a pond comes into sight at the bottom of the slope. Aim for a gate at the left end of the pond. Go through the gate and walk past the pond to cross a stile. Go half left up the field to a stile at the top of the slope. Cross the stile and keep ahead over a field to an obelisk.

This obelisk was erected in 1739 to celebrate the visit of the Prince of Wales to Banbury races, at which time he stayed at Wroxton Abbey.

❷ From the obelisk, maintain the same general direction across the field, descending towards a bridge. DO NOT cross the bridge but turn right for 10 yards, the stream on your left, to enter the next field. Go half right across the field, aiming for woods on the far side. On reaching the woods, turn left and walk along the edge of the woods, the trees on your right. At the corner, go half right across the field, passing a single nearby tree close on your left hand, and aiming for the corner of trees seen on the far side, beside a telegraph pole. Pass under the telegraph lines and then maintain the same direction across the corner of the field to the edge of a wood ahead, with a track visible beyond. Turn left and go up the farm track. Follow the track as it descends past allotments to emerge on a lane in North Newington. The Blinking Owl public house is 100 yards along to your left.

❸ Turn right and follow this quiet lane for ½ mile, ignoring a side road on the right to Wroxton. Pass the entrance drive to a house on your right, Valentine Barn. Go along the road for another 250 yards, passing the entrance to another house, until opposite a conspicuous clump of trees on top of a conical rise in the field on your left. Turn right off the road at the bridleway sign, through a metal field gate.

Go up the enclosed track, the hedge on your right and a barn on your left, to a gate. Go through and continue up the second field, still with the hedge on your right. At the top of the field go through a gate ahead. Follow a path down through the edge of the woods. At the far end, where there is a metal gate on your right, turn left and continue along the bottom edge of the woods. In 300 yards turn right through a metal gate into a field. Immediately turn left and walk along the field edge, the woods on your left.

❹ At the end of the woods, keep straight on through a gate and along an enclosed track. At the end of the first field, turn right and then left, to follow the track along the bottom of a second field. Go through the gate and keep ahead for 15 yards, then turn sharp right through a metal field gate, ignoring a waymarked gate and track ahead. Go uphill, trees on your left, to a telegraph pole. Keep ahead, following the right-hand line of telegraph poles along the side of the hill, a stream and telegraph poles in the dip to your left. As the field narrows, stay to the top edge, to reach a waymarked barrier stile near the top corner.

The bank you are walking along is the rampart of an Iron Age hillfort, a comparatively small affair built on a commanding height overlooking the surrounding countryside. It was for emergency use only, to protect the population of the neighbourhood and their livestock, who would have evacuated into the safety of the fort in times of trouble.

5 Cross the stile and follow the top of the bank as it curves left around the valley. After a line of trees on your right ends, keep ahead, passing two field gates on your right and shortly after reaching a stile on the right. Cross the stile and go three-quarters left across the field. Go through a gap in the fence into a second field, and maintain your line of advance across this field to reach a lane. Cross to a stile opposite and keep ahead along the right-hand edge of a field. At the far end, keep ahead through a pedestrian gate. Follow the right-hand edge of the field to go through another gate. Keep ahead along the side of the field.

The tower off to your right is a folly, built in the 18th century on the foundations of an earlier tower, which was part of the wall surrounding the priory.

In the bottom left corner of the field go through a kissing gate. Follow the enclosed track to a lane, and turn right back to the start.
   It is worth a short detour to visit the church. With your back to the gates of Wroxton Abbey, turn right along Church Street for 250 yards to All Saints' church.

There was already a church on this site in 1217, when the priory was founded. It was appropriated by the prior and canons for the priory's exclusive use, and from 1395 the priest in charge of the church was appointed from within the priory. The present church was largely built during the 14th century by the Priory. Inside the church is the impressive tomb of Sir William Pope, builder of Wroxton Abbey, and his family. There is also a monument to Francis, Lord Guildford, and also to Frederick, Lord North, George III's prime minister.

WALK 16
WOOLHAMPTON AND THE TRANSPORT REVOLUTION

Length: 5 miles

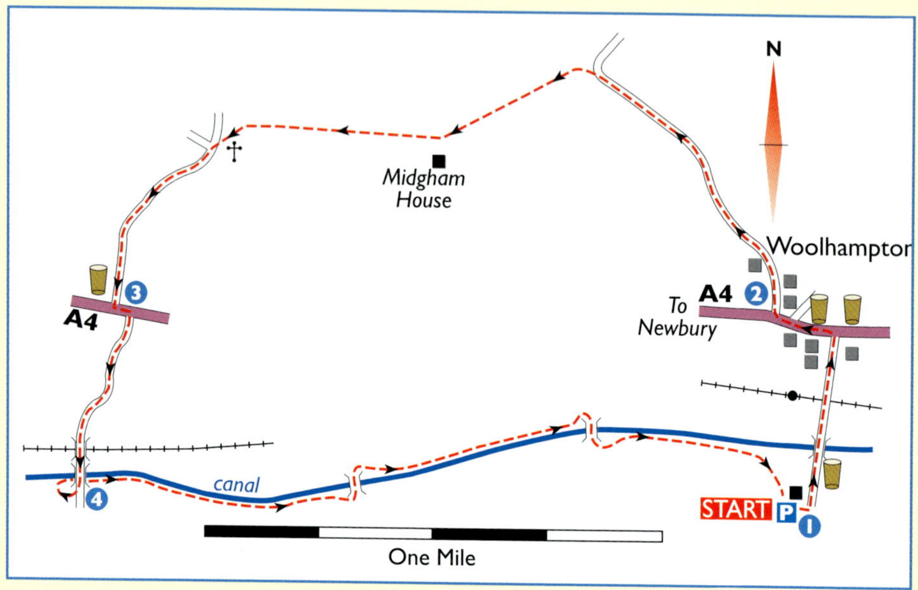

HOW TO GET THERE: This walk starts from the car park next to the Rowbarge public house in Woolhampton, on the A4, 5 miles east of Newbury.

PARKING: The free car park is on a minor road running south from the centre of Woolhampton, signed Midgham Station.

MAP: OS Landranger 174 (GR 573665).

INTRODUCTION

This walk starts at Woolhampton, climbing out of the Kennet valley to cross the grounds of Midgham House, before dropping back down into the river valley. It then follows the canal towpath back to the start. The dramatic improvements in transport known as the 'Transport Revolution' came in three main stages – roads, canals and railways – and these can all be seen in the Kennet valley around Woolhampton. Route-finding is easy, and the terrain is good underfoot and mostly flat, apart from one gradual slope up and another back down.

HISTORICAL BACKGROUND

For the industrial revolution to succeed, it was necessary for there to be a corresponding revolution in transport. The large-scale production of goods needed the means to move increasing quantities of raw materials and finished goods quickly and cheaply around the country. In the mid-18th century these means did not exist apart from around the coast. Rivers were often obstructed by weirs and fishpools, and very few could provide for the long-distance haulage of goods. Roads were of very poor quality, rutted and unsurfaced. The growth of the turnpikes – essentially private toll roads reasonably well maintained – improved the situation for passenger traffic, but they were unsuitable for moving large volumes of goods.

In 1759 a revolution in transport occurred. Francis Egerton, 2nd Duke of Bridgewater, tired of London society and disappointed in love, threw his energies into constructing a canal to connect his coalmines in Worsley to nearby Manchester. To do this Bridgewater employed James Brindley, a millwright with no formal education, who brought a natural genius to the task of civil engineering, overcame tremendous natural obstacles, and in 1761 opened the first commercial canal in England. The success of the canal as a means of moving heavy goods quickly and cheaply was immediately apparent, and the next 60 years saw canals being opened the length and breadth of Britain, in such numbers that it was described as 'canal mania'.

But canal transport was slow and there were physical limitations upon where canals could be built, and alternatives were sought. Tramways, iron rails along which laden wagons were pulled by horses, had existed in the coalfields for decades, and by 1800 horse-power was replaced by stationary steam engines winching the wagons along. The obvious next step was for the engine itself to be mobile, and the search was on to design the first 'locomotive'. Enter George Stephenson, greatest of the early railway pioneers. Stephenson, illiterate until he was 20, had a natural genius for all things mechanical. Between 1816 and 1822 Stephenson built a number of prototype steam locomotives, but the breakthrough came in 1825 when he

The canal at Midgham

designed and built a railway to carry coal from Darlington to the river port of Stockton. As well as coal, the Stockton-Darlington railway carried passengers. Four years later, Liverpool and Manchester were linked by a much larger scale railway, which generated huge profits and encouraged the development of railways all over the country. The age of the railway had arrived.

THE WALK

1   From the car park turn left along the road, passing the front of the Rowbarge, and soon crossing the canal. Follow the road over a level crossing, the station on the left, and keep ahead to reach the A4, with the Angel hotel and restaurant opposite.

The course of the main London to Bristol road has been largely unaltered since Roman times, and is followed today by the A4. The fine roads built by the Romans fell into disrepair after they left Britain in AD 410, and within a few centuries had deteriorated until little remained. There was no national authority responsible for keeping roads in good condition. By the 18th century even main roads were little more than narrow rutted tracks, reduced to quagmires of mud in wet weather.

In 1663 an Act of Parliament allowed private companies to take over the repair of roads, running them as profit-making concerns by charging tolls for their use. The roads were blocked at intervals by movable gates, or ' turnpikes', where tolls could be collected. By 1750 there were still only 400 sections of road controlled by turnpike, but changes in industry and business increased the demand for improvement. By 1790 another 1,500 turnpike trusts had been set up, and improved methods of surfacing roads, introduced by such pioneers as John MacAdam (after whom 'tarmac' is named) meant that all the major towns in England were linked by good quality roads.

The trunk road from London to Bristol road was surfaced along its whole length, with toll houses and turnpikes at regular intervals. Goods were transported by heavy wagon, whilst passengers went by high-speed stagecoach. These coaches in turn required regular 'stages', stopping points where horses could be changed and passengers could be provided with refreshments and overnight accommodation. Coaching inns thus developed at intervals along the road. The Angel Hotel started life as one such coaching inn ('The Angel' is a popular name for such establishments, with its implications of divine protection, a commodity often felt to be necessary when travelling the 18th-century roads).

Cross the A4 to the front of the Angel, and turn left to pass the front of the Falmouth Arms. Cross the side road and keep ahead along the A4 for another 30 yards, and then turn right up a lane, signed 'Midgham Green'.

2   Follow the quiet lane, passing houses and climbing steadily. At the top of the slope, where the lane bends sharp right, cross a stile on the left at a fingerpost, just to the left of an imposing concrete and wrought-iron gateway. Walk along the field, the hedge close on your right. Cross a stile and continue along the next field, now on a path, the hedge still close on your right. At the field end, cross a stile into a third field. Keep ahead along a faint path, swinging gradually right beyond trees, and dropping down to a waymarked gate.

Keep ahead across the next field to a wooden gate clearly visible on the far side. Cross a drive and go through the metal field gate opposite. Keep ahead along a track, eventually enclosed, finally leaving the track and keeping ahead along a footpath. Pass bungalows to reach gates leading into a lane, at a gate to Midgham church.

Keep ahead down the lane to reach the A4.

The Coach and Horses pub on your right is, as its name implies, another stagecoach inn from the turnpike days.

3 Cross the A4 with care, turn left and almost immediately bear right into Brimpton Road. Follow the road for ¼ mile. Cross a railway bridge and 30 yards later reach the canal. Cross the canal bridge and immediately turn right down to the towpath, at a lock. Immediately turn right again to follow the towpath under the bridge.

As soon as Bridgewater's first canal was opened in 1761, the potential for canals as a means of economically moving heavy goods quickly and cheaply was recognized. During the next 60 years canals were constructed piecemeal the length and breadth of Britain. For each canal to be built a joint stock company had to be created to raise the finance, with the return on the investment coming from its commercial operation. Such was the glamour of this latest technology that private investors flocked to the canal companies, with little thought that canals were not guaranteed money-makers.

As the 19th century dawned, Britain was already well served by a network of interconnecting canals which criss-crossed most of England, moving raw materials into the industrial cities of the north, and finished goods from those cities to the ports. Despite this, in 1810 it was decided to dig a canal to connect the river Avon at Bath with the river Kennet at Newbury, which in turn was already linked to the Thames. Thus the ports of Bristol and London were directly linked for the first time, and for 30 years the Kennet and Avon canal was a great success financially. Traffic flowed, returns on investment poured in, and the towns and villages along the route of the canal prospered.

4 Follow the towpath, eventually crossing the canal at a rotating bridge and then resuming your former direction, now on the opposite bank.

Follow the towpath past another lock, with a turning circle just beyond. Shortly afterwards cross the canal again, at a second rotating bridge.

The railway line is just on the other side of the canal, and runs parallel to it (and to the old turnpike) along the Kennet valley. The success of the Stockton to Darlington, opened in 1829, had shown that heavy goods could be transported more quickly and for less money than by canals. Financiers who had previously invested in building canals now switched their investments into railways. In 1833 the Great Western Railway Company (GWR) was founded, to build a rail link between London and Bristol, employing as its chief engineer the young but already highly respected, Isambard Kingdom Brunel.

The first train ran along the completed railway in 1838. Passenger traffic switched away from the canals and the turnpike almost immediately, and freight traffic over the next few years as the commercial advantages of the railway became apparent. Despite this, the canal continued to be a viable means of moving bulk freight, and ran successfully in direct competition with its new high-tech neighbour for the next decade. Consequently business on the railway failed to grow as fast as its stockholders would like. By 1852 the GWR had to accept that it would not be able to take business from the Kennet and Avon canal, and so instead made a successful take-over bid for the canal company. For the next 25 years the GWR ran both railway and canal in parallel, but gradually, as the railways improved in capacity and reliability, freight customers switched to rail. 1877 was the last year the Kennet and Avon canal made a profit, and within 20 years it had effectively ceased to operate commercially.

Resume your former direction, now with the canal on your right. Pass a third lock. Immediately afterwards, cross a wooden bridge over the canal.

By 1951 the Kennet and Avon canal was derelict, silted up, with banks collapsed in many places, dry for some stretches, and abandoned. But although canals were no longer viable for moving goods or passengers, a new era was dawning, when their usefulness for leisure boating was realized. By a massive effort, much of it voluntary, the Kennet and Avon canal was put back into working order. Today it is navigable for its full length and flourishes again, with narrow boats, the direct heirs of the old 19th-century barges, plying the waterways all year around.

Keep ahead along the towpath, back to the Rowbarge.

REFRESHMENTS

The Rowbarge public house at the start of the walk has a range of food and beers, and open air seating next to the canal. Telephone: 01189 712213.